In Her Shoes

Charlotte Scanlon-Gambill

Abundant Life Publishing

© Charlotte Scanlon-Gambill 2008

Abundant Life Publishing
Wapping Road, Bradford
West Yorkshire BD3 0EQ

Charlotte Scanlon-Gambill has asserted her right under the Copyright, Designs and Patents Act, 1988, to be identified as Author of this work.

All rights reserved. No part of this publication may be reproduced, stored in a retrieval system, or transmitted, in any form or by any means, electronic, mechanical, photocopying, recording or otherwise, without the prior permission of the publisher or the Copyright Licensing Agency.

Unless otherwise stated, scripture quotations are from the Holy Bible, New International Version, Copyright © 1973, 1978, 1984 International Bible Society, published by Hodder and Stoughton.

The contributors of the personal stories in this book have agreed to their use in the form as published. Their stories remain accurate but some names have been changed as appropriate for personal privacy.

First Published in 2008

British Library Cataloguing in Publication Data:
A catalogue record for this book is available from the British Library

ISBN 13 978-0-9555804-3-7

Dedication

I dedicate this book to the true heroes of the Faith. Those who have not just lived life from their own vantage point but have stepped into the shoes of others and made a difference to another's world.

To you who have loved the unlovely, embraced the unwanted, remembered the forgotten and included the lonely; you are amazing. Your reward is truly stored up in heaven but whilst you are here on earth I salute you for your strength, tenacity and selfless love. It is breathtaking.

The world is all the richer because of who you are and all you do and I pray that as you refresh others you yourself will be refreshed. I pray you will feel the kiss of heaven all over your life in increasing measure.

Much Love

Charlee

'If your heart is crying out to have a greater compassion and genuine understanding for others whose lives you may not understand, then this book is a must read. 'In Her Shoes' is the most compelling and challenging book yet for believers to love unconditionally and let mercy triumph over judgment. You will discover in very practical ways how this can become a lifestyle that is much easier than you may think, and the results will astound you!'

Nancy Alcorn
Founder and President
Mercy Ministries International

'I wish I could bottle Charlotte and take her round churches with me! She 'gets' walking in other people's shoes. I saw that during a visit with Charl and her family to Mombasa, Kenya. She was greatly moved by the poverty we confronted and as a result has helped Compassion find many hundreds of sponsors to give children in poverty the opportunity of a better future. Quite simply she saw the need and got it done. I commend Charl's 'In Her Shoes' to you; she's the real deal and I thank God for her.'

Ian Hamilton
CEO
Compassion UK

'Charlotte has done it again, writing a book that hits me right where I'm living, offering insightful, practical and spiritual applications for everyday life. This book challenges me to get my eyes off my own shoes and look for opportunities to step into someone else's. Thank you friend, for showing me that although I may think the shoes of another might not be my style or fashion, they will end up being the perfect fit, as I take the time to walk in her shoes.'

Natalie Grant
Dove Award Winner
Female Vocalist

Contents

Chapter 1   In Her Shoes

Chapter 2   The Power Of Context

Chapter 3   Once Upon A Time

Chapter 4   Leaving Neverland

Chapter 5   What's Your Shoe Size?

Chapter 6   First Things First

Chapter 7   What Can You Do?

Chapter 8   Stepping Out

Chapter 9   In Their Shoes

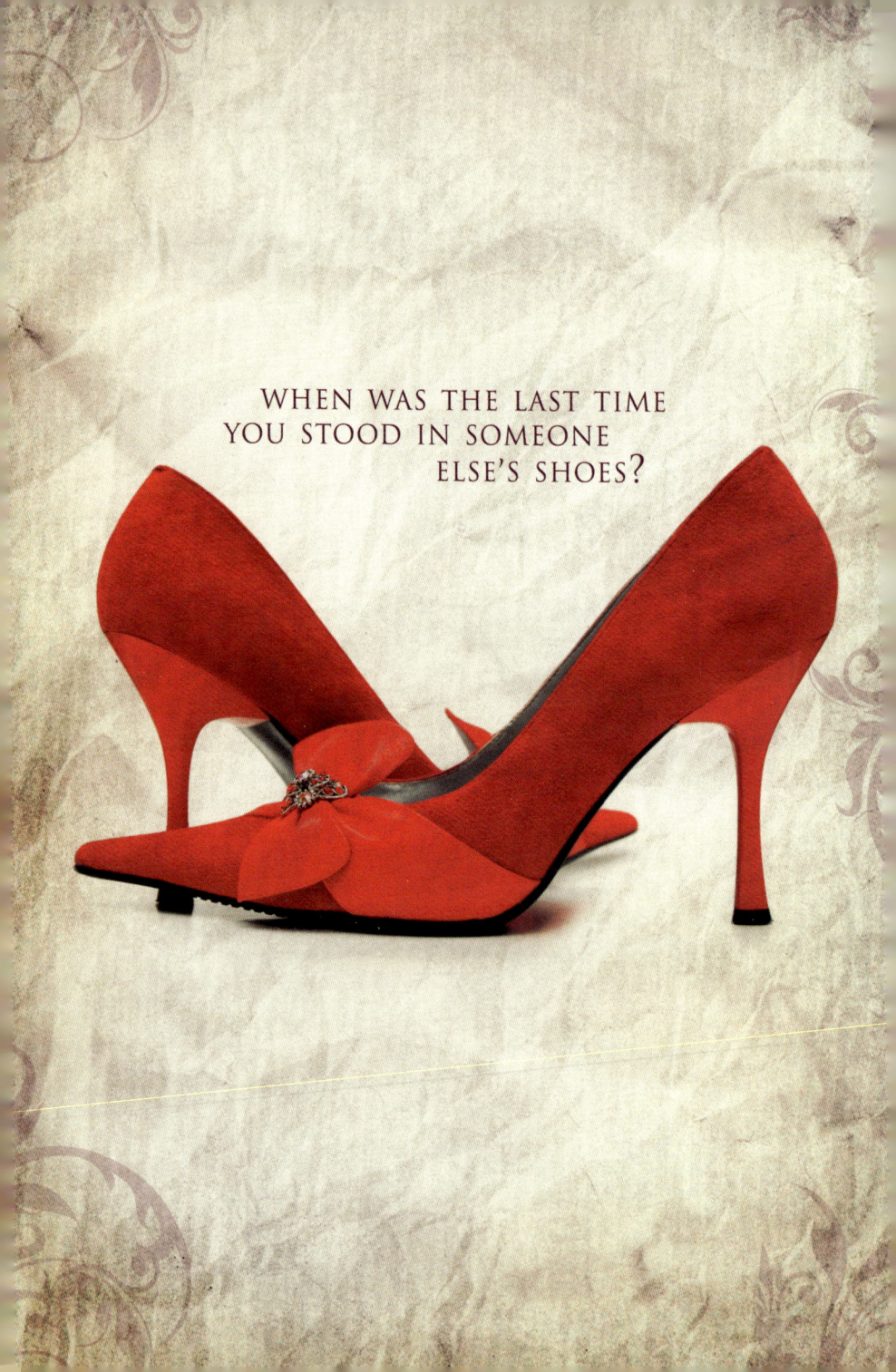

WHEN WAS THE LAST TIME
YOU STOOD IN SOMEONE
ELSE'S SHOES?

CHAPTER 1

IN HER SHOES

Have you ever been into a shoe shop and tried to find that perfect pair of shoes? You see a vast array of different styles and colours in front of you and your attention is soon taken by a stunning pair of bright red stilettos with a four inch heel - well mine is anyway! Most women love a good shoe shop but I often wonder why we seem to find a sense of happiness in trying on lots of shoes. After carefully surveying each shelf we try on shoes we have no intention of buying, anything from a cute flat pump to a ridiculously tall, towering heel. We then pretend we are bold enough to buy those six inch pink stilettos, but usually end up settling for something far more practical. The experience we have in the shoe shop is the same experience we need to embrace throughout our life. We must be willing to try on the shoes of many different people, from the shoes of the single mum to the shoes of the orphan child; and from the shoes of the glamorous business woman to the shoes of the elderly. When we step into the shoes of others and say, "I'll try to walk in these," we deepen our empathy, begin to stretch our heart and enlarge our world.

This book has been written to encourage you to do just that and learn to stand in the shoes of others. This lost world needs a relevant church with compassion and genuine understanding for the lives of others. They don't want a church that wags a judgemental finger at people as they walk past. We need to show people that God's love is gracious, compassionate and relevant to them. So let me ask you, when was the last time you stood in someone else's shoes?

Passers By

There is a pretty village near to where I live, set in the picturesque Yorkshire countryside. It's a favourite place of mine and I love to visit one of the many outdoor cafes that line the streets on a sunny afternoon. As I sit there with my latte, I find it fascinating to watch people as they go about their daily lives.

In Her Shoes

Different people catch my eye. First of all I notice an old lady sat on a bench with her shopping trolley parked next to her. I watch as she dozes in the afternoon sunshine and start to wonder if she has a family, or whether she is alone in life. Suddenly she is disturbed from her snooze by a young boy skateboarding past on the side walk. You can tell that many of the passers by think he is an inconsiderate teenager by the disapproving looks they throw in his direction.

My attention eventually rests on a young mum and I smile at how much extra stuff being a mother requires you to carry. She is kitted out with an array of bags, strollers and accessories to keep the kids entertained and cater for every eventuality. I watch her as she tries to negotiate with a screaming child over the fact that they cannot have a second ice cream, as an almighty wail starts to erupt from her other child in the stroller. She looks harassed and tries her best to silence their cries, feeling embarrassed that her kids are now attracting an audience for their noisy performance.

As I sit there child free and working on my laptop our worlds look like they have nothing in common. She catches my eye for a moment and then turns her attention back to her children. In those few seconds she has probably decided that our lives are totally different. Perhaps she assumes that I am single with no children to bother my peaceful day and that I can't relate to her stress. But as a mother, I can sympathise with her dilemma of having too many children and too few hands to keep hold of them. Her assumptions like many of ours are based on what she sees and our lives remain disconnected from each other although we may actually have a lot in common.

This same scenario plays out hundreds of times every day. Often we can base our perception of what people are like on what we see or have heard without stopping to find out anything meaningful about their story. The fact is you can't tell where anyone is at in life by looking at what you see on the outside. To truly understand someone you have to take the time to dig deeper. What you discover can often surprise you because the person who you thought had a perfect life may secretly be falling apart. Or the woman who seems to be super confident may actually be struggling with low self esteem. The point is we just don't know what is going on underneath the surface of someone's life until we get to know them.

In Her Shoes

We are all called to reach others. This is a mandate that God has placed on each of our lives without exception. But sometimes we have made this far more complicated than it should be. We think that to win people over we have to impress them, or have all the right answers to any difficult questions they might ask. This can leave us feeling that we are under-qualified for the task. In reality most people are easier to reach than that. All they want is for someone to stop and care enough to give them the precious commodity of their time. Many people are tired of feeling isolated and are looking for a point of connection, for empathy and for someone to understand what it is like to live their life. All they want is for someone to step into their shoes.

Walking In Other Shoes

Jesus modelled a life that was determined and very deliberate about walking in the shoes of others. He could have come to chastise, challenge and judge people for their lifestyles but instead he committed to love them. He took time to engage with their lives and display compassion and understanding. Jesus did this by connecting with people wherever they were doing life. He never barged in with his words but measured them carefully and then spoke into each life in the most appropriate manner.

He said, *'For I did not come to judge the world, but to save it'* *(John 12:47)*. We need a commitment in every believer's heart to approach life in the same way. To connect with others and be people who are not afraid to walk a mile in someone else's shoes.

Jesus never watered down his answers to people and he was not soft on the sin he encountered. He sought to gently restore them not condemn them. By stepping into their shoes he was able to wrap his confrontation or correction in compassion for their situation and grace for their circumstances. The Gospels are full of stories about Jesus creating life-changing moments for those he met by stepping into their shoes. Often they were people that others had already judged and refused to reach out to. Let's consider a few of those encounters.

The Man Up A Tree

To most people in the city of Jericho, Zacchaeus was a despised tax collector and crook. But one day Jesus walked by and caught a glimpse of him straining to get a good view from his tree-top hideout. As he stepped into his shoes Jesus saw Zacchaeus in a totally different way to everyone else. He saw a lost and lonely man who had made many mistakes and was searching for answers. He saw someone who had been dishonest and was now ostracised by a community who had become his judge and jury. Jesus didn't condone Zacchaeus' sin that day but instead felt his shame and reached out to him.

Just imagine that you were an outcast like Zacchaeus. What would most impact your world? How about the very person everyone else wanted to be with noticing you and inviting himself to your house for dinner. It was the ultimate act of acceptance. With that one gesture Jesus challenged the lack of compassion in others and showed Zacchaeus that he wasn't being judged. This display of empathy and understanding led Zacchaeus to repentance and as a result he became a changed man. One simple act of stepping into his shoes achieved what pointing out his failings never could.

The Woman At The Well

There was the time when Jesus met one woman at a well. Others in the community disapproved of her lifestyle so they gossiped about her and ignored her. They had already decided what sort of woman she was and had judged her harshly. But when Jesus sat next to her and stepped into her shoes he looked at her through different eyes to everyone else. He sensed her brokenness and the rejection and pain that overwhelmed her life. Jesus saw her fruitless and unfulfilled search for love. Instead of condemning her he gently led her to a place of healing and restoration. I read this story and asked myself what I would have done. Would I have kept my distance or stepped into her shoes? We all have to ask ourselves the same question because no-one can be helped when we stand on the sidelines with nothing to offer but our disapproving looks. The best help comes from a person who has first stepped into the shoes of others.

The Hungry Crowd

Jesus had thousands of people listening to him teach one day when he suddenly stopped because of his concern for their well-being. Perhaps it was because he heard a few stomachs rumbling and felt the blistering heat of the sun on their heads. His heart was moved to help them so he asked the disciples who was going to feed the hungry crowd, but they didn't feel it was their responsibility. After all they were there to heal the sick and do miracles, not provide a packed lunch service. But Jesus had stepped into the shoes of the crowd and they weren't just a sea of faces to him. He saw individual men, women and children who were hungry and thirsty. They had physical needs that he could tend to. Jesus never got so caught up in what he was doing that he forgot who he was doing it for. He was never more concerned with impressing the crowd than meeting their needs and his gesture that day demonstrated his commitment to be mindful of what it was like to be in their shoes.

Tears For Lazarus

When Lazarus died Jesus wept with Mary and Martha, even though he was going to raise him from the dead a few moments later. Crying seems like a strange thing to do, especially when he could have marched straight in there and performed a great miracle without having to shed a single tear. Maybe we would have waded in as the hero to save the day, but Jesus stopped and stepped into the shoes of those two women who were grieving for their brother. He felt their loss, he identified with them and shared their pain despite knowing that their tears of sadness would soon be turned to tears of joy.

I could go on because there are so many stories where Jesus got alongside people and demonstrated his commitment to walk for a while in their shoes. Jesus loved people, he understood them. When they were with him, they knew they were in the safe hands of someone who cared and would not condemn them. Jesus walked in the shoes of others so he could laugh with them, cry with them, feel their pain and celebrate their success. We are called to do exactly the same.

The Joy Of Connecting

Once we start to adjust our focus away from our own lives and onto others we will see the need for us to slow down and reach out. It may not always be convenient but you will soon discover that there is something very beautiful that comes from stopping, and there is a special joy that is only found when we decide to connect.

Recently I was travelling by train across the UK. I bought a ticket for the most direct route with a non-stop service so I could reach my destination as quickly as possible. The journey there was fast, we went through many stations and I saw many people stood on the platform waiting for a train, but we didn't give them the option to get on board.

In Her Shoes

We were on a mission, our destination and schedule was set and there was no time to stop. However, on the way home the direct service was unavailable, so my journey became a much longer three and half hour trip with multiple stops. I remember being very annoyed that more and more people were getting on board the train. What had been a comfortable journey with plenty of space, was becoming cramped as the extra passengers took up the seats around me. My quiet, empty carriage was now noisy and crammed full of people who were disturbing my journey. As I sat there, I felt God remind me of my first train ride on the way there and ask which journey was most like my life, and which like his. Would Jesus whizz past the waiting passengers, too busy to stop? Would he be so caught up in his own journey that he wouldn't engage with others wanting to get on board and travel with him? Or would he allow himself to be inconvenienced for the sake of those around him?

Jesus built a life that made many stops. He opened the doors of his life and let others climb on board with him. He welcomed all potential passengers and was often surrounded by chaos with people pressing him on every side, just like I was on the train that day. Yet his attitude and mine couldn't have been more different because what he saw as a sea of need and opportunity, I saw as a sea of inconvenience and a nuisance. He entered people's worlds and was never too busy to walk in their shoes. He had many ways of opening the door of his life so they could climb on board. What about you?

Embracing Others

One year at our annual Cherish women's conference in Bradford, I decided to enter the world of some special girls by throwing a massive baby shower for pregnant teenagers. I wrote to all the conference delegates asking them to bring a brand new baby item to give away. We contacted all of the agencies in our city who work with pregnant teenagers and asked if they knew any girls who would like to come. We wanted to celebrate the baby they had chosen to carry and cheer them on at a time when they probably felt the disapproval of many in their world. When we stepped into their shoes we didn't see teenagers who had made a stupid mistake. We saw girls who were lost, girls who felt very lonely and scared as they faced up to the challenges of pending motherhood. The Cherish girls were amazing and went crazy buying presents for girls they would never actually meet and for babies that they would never hold. It was our way of joining together as a group of women and saying, 'We believe in you! We don't want to judge you, we want to support you!'

That night before the meeting started, I sat in the balcony of our main auditorium to see the gifts before anyone arrived. I just wept as I saw over seven thousand items that had been donated, each one saying, 'We don't judge you, we love you.' There were strollers, cots, sterilizers, clothes, nappies, bedding, toys, highchairs and everything you could possibly need for a new baby. We filled the stage with all the beautiful gifts and turned it into a nursery. It looked amazing and we asked each woman who brought something to write an encouraging message to go with their present. When the teenage girls arrived that night they looked a little overwhelmed as they sat in the service and we were so aware that they could have felt uncomfortable. Maybe they expected to be judged. What they were not prepared for was to be understood or that we would take the time to walk in their shoes. As they sat there we loved them, extended grace to them and I read out the following story:

In Her Shoes

"I got pregnant when I was 16, my boyfriend and I were terrified, it was an accident, it wasn't planned or wanted. The consequences were awful. I had just left school, he was still at school and we had no money, no jobs, nowhere to live and no one to turn to.

The thought of telling my parents something so devastating was unbearable. I had a great Mum and Dad and I hated hurting them so much. They had trusted me with this boy and I had betrayed them, this was not what they had ever imagined for their little girl. Our lives were plunged into months of pain, days of fear, worry, regret and worst of all we felt so isolated and an overwhelming sense of loneliness. We didn't know who to turn to. I remember so clearly the feeling of being trapped. This was not the life I wanted, it was not what I had dreamed about.

We were both just 16, we were kids, teenagers. We should have been out with our mates enjoying our youth. Instead we were about to take on the biggest responsibility in life. We didn't know what to do, we had no idea how to care for a baby we were not ready for this but it was too late. All my plans to go on to further studies were cut short, my boyfriend left school and got the only job he could as a *labourer on a building site. He hated that job and I hated watching what it did to him. He was only a boy but had to become a man fast, too fast. We lived apart for months whilst I was pregnant, I was at home with my parents. Neither of our parents spoke to each other about what had happened.*

I remember the day when the baby was born; here we were, kids holding a kid. We now had this life to think about, to provide for, and to care for. It was overwhelming. We eventually got married aged 16 and 17. My boyfriend's father didn't even come to our wedding because he was so ashamed of us. We had nowhere to live so we moved into my parents' spare bedroom. The three of us lived in that cramped room for the next nine months. I don't know how we stayed together but we did, we loved each other and our baby and lived a day at a time.

My husband started going to a church youth group and he began to change, and it was a good change. Months later I started going with him to church and we both gave our lives to God. Sadly, our decision to follow God estranged us even more from our families at a time when we most needed them.

In Her Shoes

Looking back the church became our family, it saved our lives and our baby girl grew up in God's house. She has never lived a day of her life outside of the family of God, and I know that was our saving grace. Because of that my story of being a teenage mum has a happy ending as I now carry on writing my story, happily married with my family and grandchildren around me.

This is my story, my name is Glenda Scanlon and my boyfriend's name was Paul Scanlon. The unplanned baby girl reading this story to you today is my eldest daughter Charlotte."

This is my Mum's amazing story. She was once a pregnant teenager herself and knew what it was like to be looked down on by society. My Mum and Dad had faced the same struggle to bring me up when they were little more than children themselves. Her story helped her make a precious connection with each girl as she stepped into their shoes and said 'don't give up, you can do this, we believe in you!' That night we saw a glimpse of heaven as many women from totally different backgrounds showed compassion towards those girls. It was a precious moment and as a result some of those girls gave their lives to Jesus and this was the ultimate gift we could have given their unborn child. I felt God's smile all over us that evening as we touched his heart for those girls.

It is such an amazing privilege to step into other people's shoes. This simple act can open the door for God to change people's lives. Our world is full of people who are alone, they feel misunderstood and are waiting for someone to care enough to lead them forward. We need to enlarge our heart and deepen our compassion to understand the challenges faced by people from all different walks of life.

This book is written to encourage you to go into the 'shoe shop' of your community or wherever you do life, and try on the shoes of other people just like Jesus did. Together we will consider the cost involved, the way living this kind of life will challenge our priorities and place more demand on our personal growth. In the final chapter you will find the stories of many amazing women who have walked very different journeys. Each one has extended a generous invitation for you to learn more about their life and their experiences. As you walk in their shoes for a while, I pray God will deepen your love for others and spur you on.

In Her Shoes

So that you will reach out to the many people who are longing for someone to walk in their shoes, and will teach them how to walk in his.

WHO ARE YOU WILLING TO SWAP SHOES WITH?

Homeless

CHAPTER 2

THE POWER OF CONTEXT

All of us are living life within a particular context. It is the background scenery to our lives which adds colour and shade to our perspective. It is an explanation for why we feel the way we do and it plays a vital part in shaping the decisions we make. It is the lens that we see life through and the angle that alters our perspective. If we want to learn to walk in the shoes of other people then we must start to embrace the context of people's lives. It will prevent us from rushing into situations and making rash judgements without first finding out both sides of the story. Context is very powerful but often it isn't even taken into account.

I used to make assumptions about others all the time and say things like, 'It's alright for them!' Or I would judge people from a distance until I started to understand

In Her Shoes

context. Once I immersed myself in their world I discovered that what I had judged with a momentary glance was actually a very complicated situation with a history that had helped to create it. As I began to consider the background scenery of people's lives it helped me relate in a more appropriate manner. I started to comprehend why they said certain things or reacted in particular ways and this helped to inform my own contribution to their world. Context became a useful guide that could steer any wisdom and advice that I sought to bring.

Embracing context places you in the world of the person you are trying to reach. You don't just see a woman but a busy mother who is stressed out, it allows for her distracted state and frazzled nerves. It stops you from seeing a boisterous, unruly teenager and paints a bigger picture which shows the challenges they face in overcoming peer pressure and their insecurities. Without embracing context we can end up labelling people with the usual stereotypes and moving on. But we are called to be a friend of sinners, a bringer of good news and when we gain context it helps us to do this more effectively.

In Her Shoes

There's Always Two Sides

Actions without context can be like the dad who returns home to see his son sitting crying on the step. He flings his arms around his son to console him, wipes away the tears and much to the boy's delight he gives him a piggy back ride up the stairs. As they enter the kitchen together the context of those tears starts to unfold. A tired, stressed out mother is sweeping broken glass from the floor and a football is next to her. Context explains why the child was sitting on the step that day, it fills in the missing details and now the dad sees a complete picture of the events that day for the first time. In an instant, his perspective has changed as he feels sympathy for his wife and disappointment towards his son. Meanwhile his wife is cross with him for making light of such a serious discipline issue.

This is what our lives are like. Every person has background scenery and you can't understand it clearly until you walk in their shoes. How often do we rush in to comfort the equivalent of the crying boy in our world and put ourselves in the middle of a situation before finding out both sides to the story? We can be too quick to offer our advice without first asking some questions. Or we can lead the charge to right a wrong for an upset friend without first making sure their complaint is valid.

It says in Proverbs, *'The first to present his case seems right, till another comes forward and questions him' (Proverbs 18:17).* These wise words from King Solomon encourage us to step back and survey the scene before deciding our response.

A Wise Woman

There is a story in 2 Samuel which paints a great picture of the power of context at work. Joab was the military leader of David's army and his men were hunting for a fugitive who had rebelled against the king. They were about to storm the city of Sheba where they thought the man was hiding. Joab was so focused on his mission that his concern was simply to kill this man and everything else was an insignificant detail. He was single-minded in his aim and yet this rampage meant taking the lives of many innocent people. As they were about to storm the city one brave woman managed to stop Joab and his men in their tracks. She gave them some context by explaining the history of the place they were about to destroy.

In Her Shoes

It says, 'All the troops with Joab came and besieged Sheba in Abel Beth Maacah. They built a siege ramp up to the city and it stood against the outer fortifications. While they were battering the wall to bring it down, a wise woman called from the city, "Listen! Listen! Tell Joab to come here so I can speak to him." He went towards her, and she asked, "Are you Joab?" "I am," he answered. She said, "Listen to what your servant has to say." "I am listening" he said. She continued, "Long ago they used to say, 'Get your answer at Abel,' and that settled it. We are the peaceful and faithful in Israel. You are trying to destroy a city that is a mother in Israel. Why do you want to swallow up the Lord's inheritance?'

(2 Samuel 20:15-19)

Can you picture the scene? Thousands of troops were on the rampage, battering down the city gates and in the midst of the chaos a woman says, 'Excuse me, can I have a word! I'm not quite sure why you are doing this, but I think you need to understand where you are before you destroy it!' She explained that if they had bothered to find out anything about the town, they would have known it had a reputation for peace, not war. This woman wanted to know why they were trying to barge their way in, she

In Her Shoes

wanted them to explain their actions to her. A great army commander was stopped in his tracks by a woman saying 'Hey are you Joab? I know you are on a mission but we need to have a little chat before you ruin our lives. Please can we talk and work out the best way to deal with this situation?'

By talking to Joab, the woman gave him the opportunity to explain the context of his situation to her. She stepped into his shoes and in return he stepped into hers.

Joab explained saying, ' *"A man named Sheba son of Bicri, from the hill country of Ephraim, has lifted up his hand against the king, against David. Hand over this one man, and I'll withdraw from this city." The woman said to Joab, "His head will be thrown to you from the wall." Then the woman went to all the people with her wise advice, and they cut off the head of Sheba son of Bicri and threw it to Joab. So he sounded the trumpet, and his men dispersed from the city, each returning to his home.'*

(2 Samuel 20:21-22)

All it took to resolve the situation was a conversation. The information that Joab gained gave him new insight into where he was and understanding the context saved many lives that day. The only person who died was the bad guy. It's so easy for us to do the equivalent of what Joab and his men did that day. Their heart and actions were right, they were going after the enemy of the king, but their approach needed adapting. They didn't need to rush in and lop off the heads of everyone living there, they just needed to say, 'Can we talk about this?'

Compassion Deficit

I have had too many Joab moments when needless energy was wasted on things that were not even the problem. Wrong calls are made and innocent people get hurt when we fail to stop and survey the scenery surrounding the challenges we face. I remember this happening when I had first started out in ministry and was asked to speak to our Welcome Team about punctuality and a few other issues. I was very young and eager to prove myself, so the next day I called the team together and gave them a very strong reprimand. I told them how they were letting the rest of the church down by not being there on time, I pointed out how irresponsible their behaviour was and gave a very eloquent but firm rebuke. I left feeling like I'd done a great job because I had made it very clear what was expected of them.

The next day I was called into the office. Instead of being congratulated for handling the situation so well, I was told that over half of the Welcome Team had resigned. I realised that unless I went and apologised, I would be greeting people on the door, helping to park cars and taking the offering by myself on Sunday. I have to admit that I did try to figure out how that would work logistically, because it seemed like a better option than having to swallow my pride and make an apology. That day I was given a powerful lesson, a lesson about context. I felt challenged as I realised what it was like to be in the shoes of the people I had spoken to. Some of them had to catch three buses to get to church, but I had a car. Others were mums who got up extra early to get their children ready so that they could be there but I was single at the time. Others were students with unreliable transport arrangements, and all of them were volunteers but I was a paid member of staff. Instead of taking a moment to step into their shoes I had made a judgement that lacked understanding. No-one minds a challenge if they feel your compassion, even a rebuke can be welcomed when you take context into account. People can feel helped and understood at the same time as being provoked and corrected when you first walk in their shoes.

This experience made me realise my life had a compassion deficit and I began to look at the situations that accompanied the lives of others. As I started to do this the power of context began to shape my words and enrich my actions. This is a challenge that I am still committed to working on today. I want to build a wise and compassionate life, one that isn't too busy to stop and understand people. Learning to embrace context and walk in the shoes of others continues to enrich my life immeasurably and it will do the same for you.

Cherish Foundation

A few years ago, I felt God whisper an idea in my heart that would be an opportunity for some people to express this practically. The Cherish Foundation was birthed and has become an amazing part of our annual Cherish women's conference. It creates an opportunity for us to walk in the shoes of some very special women. Together we listen to some amazing stories of people who have

In Her Shoes

journeyed through some incredible tests and trials. Women who have overcome cancer, have survived betrayal, abuse or been left to raise their children alone in difficult circumstances. Others who have overcome disability or achieved what people said was not possible. As a DVD of each award winner's story is played, we learn about what it is like to live their life and together we celebrate their tenacity, strength and perseverance. As we hear and connect with their story our hearts are moved.

Each year on the last night of the Cherish conference we give some incredible gifts to these women. We give away cars, holidays, home makeovers or something that will make a big difference to their lives. It is our way of saying 'We love you, we believe in you, we are standing beside you in your shoes to applaud you.' None of the women have any idea they are getting an award until their name is read out. They are totally shocked and can't believe how much others care about them. The look on their face as they make their way to the stage is priceless.

The Cherish Foundation is precious for many reasons, but one of the main things I love about it is that we all stop for a moment and enter the world of other people. We uncover the context of their lives and see the surrounding scenery. As we see them standing strong despite the difficult situations they face we don't just see a woman doing life anymore. Now we see a mum who has the perseverance of a superhero and the faith of a warrior. Or we see an elderly lady who has been one of life's survivors. Every year as the Cherish Foundation takes place, tears fall and joy rises as we all gain a new empathy for someone else's life, and I love it!

Who don't you understand? Whose world seems too difficult for you to enter? There will always be people we find it harder to connect with but context can put their lives into perspective for us. It provides a door through which we can reach into the world of others and creates a new entrance point into their lives. Jesus understood its power because it gave him a way to open up people's hearts and speak right into their situations. It helped him place the right words in the right settings. It says in Proverbs, *'A word aptly spoken is like apples of gold in settings of silver'* (Proverbs 25:11).

In Her Shoes

You may have experienced times when the words that came out of your mouth were not very helpful because they were ill-fitting and badly timed. Or maybe you have been on the receiving end of such words. Context helps us to address this. It gives us the ability to choose our words more carefully and makes them become all the more beautiful and pleasant to the hearer.

The truth is there are so many people to reach, we cannot sit back and think we don't need to step into someone else's shoes. Sometimes we just need to be willing to stop, open up our life and make a connection with the people around us. That is all that the woman did in Sheba that day, she simply told Joab the story of her city and her people. If she had said, 'I can't speak to Joab. I'm just a woman and I have no idea how to relate to an Army Commander!' then many lives would have been lost. Instead she shared her concerns, she told her story and invited Joab to step into her shoes and she stepped into his. You can do the same and your story is a great way to start sharing the context of your life. It was one of Jesus' favourite ways of opening the door of his life and is a tool that can help us learn to walk a few more miles in other people's shoes.

YOUR STORY ALLOWS
OTHERS TO SHARE
YOUR JOURNEY

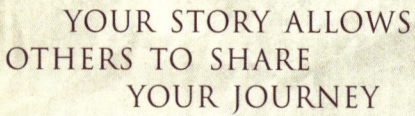

IT INVITES THEM TO
TRY ON YOUR SHOES

CHAPTER 3

ONCE UPON A TIME

The power of storytelling is something that has been used for generations as a connection point between people. Even in everyday life our conversations are full of stories about what we have done, the people we do life with, our hopes and our dreams.

My world is very alive with the power of storytelling because I have two young adorable kids. This tried and tested tradition of connecting has become a daily activity in our family. No matter how busy our day has been, every night is the same for them. Once they go to bed it's story time. Even though the deal is that they have one book read to them, it often stretches to two or three as we lose track of time in the ballroom with Cinderella, or at the dwarves' house with Snow White. We visit the jungle with Mowgli and Baloo and ride back on the flying carpet with Aladdin. These stories are shaping our children's thinking. So much truth is hidden within them and they contain many lessons for us all to learn. Like don't wear glass slippers because they can break when you most need them, or if you call at Grandma's house and she seems to have a lot of facial hair and very sharp teeth then it might not be your Grandma! But on a more serious note, children do find truths in age old stories. It's one of the first places they learn about right and wrong and good versus evil. They learn that kindness is something to be sought after and that there is power in a believing heart.

Stories are powerful, they can move your emotions, expand your imagination and make you laugh or cry. Some stories can have you on the edge of your seat with excitement as the plot unfolds, or can make you angry at the injustice they portray, others warm your heart and restore your hope in people.

The Ultimate Storyteller

Jesus understood the power of storytelling, he saw that it could help people relate to his life and journey. Although he only had three years of public ministry before he went to the cross, he chose to invest much of his precious time in storytelling. Jesus wanted to connect as many people as possible to God's power and this was one of the most effective ways of doing that. Stories were an easy way for people to climb on board Jesus' life and learn from him.

Large crowds of people followed Jesus everywhere he went, they gathered to listen to his stories. He took time to tell parables, sometimes one after another to ensure that all those within the sound of his voice could get on board. If he didn't connect with them at the first stop then he would try again at the next. Jesus used stories to tell profound truths. He dressed up life changing wisdom in accessible anecdotes, and words of correction and challenge in colour and imagery. When the crowd listened to Jesus, they didn't feel the rebuke but felt they had benefited from understanding the lesson. He told funny stories, clever stories, moving stories. He never just preached at people, he loved them and won them over with his storytelling gift. But this skill of simply telling our story and an understanding of the power it holds has somehow been lost to the church.

It says in Revelation 12, *'They overcame him by the blood of the Lamb and by the word of their testimony'*

(Revelation 12:11)

In Her Shoes

This verse is a picture of the power source of the cross, and the connection point with our story and these two elements were meant to work together. The Church has often separated this winning combination causing it to become less effective in reaching others. When we demonstrate the power of the cross through our story, it clearly shows how his divine power and sacrifice is at work in our everyday lives. By turning on a light switch you can illuminate an entire room. This is what happens when we have the power of God and our story working in tandem, it causes a connection and helps others see who God is and what he is able to do in our lives.

The Power Of Stories

The great thing is everyone qualifies as a storyteller. Yet often we have made it an activity that only a few brilliant, eloquent people get to do, or we think that a testimony must be something dramatic. We end up restricting the stories told to someone testifying about the horrific life they used to have, of the drugs they used to take, of their wild living and how it all changed when they became a Christian. And while these stories allow people to see God's power, they are not where everyone lives. They will connect with certain groups of people who have also walked in those shoes. But what if the rest of those listening can't connect to that person's journey because their story is so different? Well maybe they could relate to you! Could the story of how you survived a difficult illness connect with your neighbour whose mother has cancer? What about the couple who are desperate to start a family but are struggling to get pregnant? Maybe you can connect with them.

Several years ago my husband and I were told we would never have children and we battled with infertility for years. Whenever I share that part of my story I enter the world of many women who didn't realise I could relate to their situation. I understand their barrenness and how their heart aches for a child because I have been in their shoes. My hope now becomes an inspiration to them and my triumph is their encouragement not to give up. Our similar journeys connect our lives together on a deeper level. They enable us to walk for a while in their shoes, and after walking just a few miles we can share their sadness, their joy, successes and failures.

In Her Shoes

What story can you tell to help others? You may not have had a dramatic moment when you saw an angel or heard God speak to you in an audible voice. Maybe you simply made a decision, changed something in your life and wrote another chapter of your story. Now there is valuable wisdom in your journey that someone else needs to hear.

A Long Storytelling Afternoon

Jesus' love of storytelling was something that even his disciples didn't fully understand. One account of a day in the life of Jesus says, *'All Jesus did that day was tell stories – a long storytelling afternoon' (Matthew 13:34, The Message)*. At the end of another long day watching Jesus tell stories, they eventually came to a place of frustration and possibly confusion. A large crowd had gathered to see this amazing mighty miracle worker Jesus. They had heard he could make cripples walk and the blind see, he could raise the dead and deliver people from demons. This was the Jesus the crowd had come to see and the disciples were probably embarrassed and slightly disappointed at him when he stood up in front of the crowd and began to tell stories about farmers, coins and sheep. They wanted him to prove himself and probably knew that some of

In Her Shoes

Jesus' fiercest critics who didn't believe he could perform miracles were in the crowd that day. The disciples wanted Jesus to silence any questioning minds with a demonstration of his power but instead he simply told stories. At the end of the day the disciples finally asked Jesus why he was doing this.

It says in Matthew 13, *'The disciples came up and asked, "Why do you tell stories?" He replied, "You've been given insight into God's kingdom. You know how it works. Not everybody has this gift, this insight; it hasn't been given to them. Whenever someone has a ready heart for this, the insights and understandings flow freely. But if there is no readiness, any trace of receptivity soon disappears. That's why I tell stories: to create readiness, to nudge the people toward receptive insight."'*
(Matthew 13: 10-13, The Message)

Jesus' response was amazing and very helpful for all of us who want to enter the world of other people. He told stories for two reasons; because they created readiness in the hearts of people and they also nudged them towards wanting to find out more.

In Her Shoes

Readiness And Receptivity

Readiness and receptivity are what we all desire to see in the hearts of lost and broken people. We need that sense of openness in the hearts of people that we do life with everyday. We often pray for people to be open, to be receptive, but Jesus showed that stories are a vehicle to achieve this through. For generations the church has ploughed the gospel into people, trying to force the seeds of good news into rocky, hard ground. But Jesus loved people and showed genuine concern for them, his stories connected with the human heart and he used them to build a bridge between himself and humanity. He spoke to beggars, prostitutes, tax collectors, mothers and business entrepreneurs. Jesus had far less in common with the average person on the street than you or I. He was the only person on the planet who had never sinned, but his stories helped him connect with sinners and had a purpose that went beyond simply entertaining others. His stories were a powerful key which could unlock hearts that had been closed to the good news of the gospel.

Nudge Nudge

Jesus compared the power of stories to a nudge; he said that they *'nudge the people towards receptive insight' (Matthew 13:13, The Message).* We all know what it is like to be nudged either by accident or on purpose. A nudge is a polite call for your attention; it's like someone saying, 'Hey, listen up!' It's familiar and it's not offensive. Telling a story can have the same effect as nudging someone. Jesus never pushed people; he just nudged them towards the truth until they gained real insight into who he was.

If only the church could learn to nudge people, but on the most part we have made a nudge a push and wondered why people have got so upset. No-one likes to be pushed into something, but a nudge is acceptable. It's enough to get my attention but not too much to repel me. It's time to learn from the life of Jesus and try a new approach. Quit shoving and pushing. Try a nudge, it is far more effective.

We need a fresh release of stories, we need to increase our willingness to connect with people and step in their shoes. Taking the time to stop and enter someone's world can be far more powerful than we realise.

In Her Shoes

Make a point of deliberately opening up your life to others and start thinking about how you can stop and make this happen. Your connection point doesn't have to be complicated, your story doesn't have to be presented flawlessly, it just needs to be part of who you are. It needs to be an accessible part of your journey. The more we open up the door the more opportunity we will have to share our various stories. We need to look for places where we can give away our journey and connect with others. You can make this happen on a daily basis from simply stopping to help the mum who is struggling to carry her shopping to starting up a conversation with someone on a train.

One of my favourite ways to connect is to buy the drink of the person behind me in the queue at Starbucks, as I spend a lot of time in there. Recently I did this for a teenage boy who was with his friends. They clearly had more money than him and were buying drinks and cake. No-one offered to buy him a drink and he looked embarrassed. I could see him longingly eyeing up a hot chocolate so I said, 'Hey, it's free Starbucks day. You choose and I pay!' He was shocked, but quickly got over it as any smart teenager would and he ordered several cakes and a drink. The shop manager was so amazed he took our photo for his notice board because he had never seen someone do that for a stranger. That simple step of buying someone a drink opened up a way for me to tell them some of my story about why I was in town and what I was doing. I explained that I was visiting a church in town and asked them along to some meetings.

I don't know if he ever followed through on the invite, but as we interacted that day I believe I just gave him a nudge. Now when he thinks of a preacher he will remember the lady who stopped that day to buy him a hot chocolate and chose to engage with him rather than ignore him. The connection we made that day may make him more receptive to the next person who tells him their story.

We need to open our eyes to the people around us and use every opportunity just as Jesus did. Make nudging a regular part of your life, think of ways you can give your story away to others and open up the door to your world. What can you do to nudge someone today?

The Lending Library

Do you realise how many people are stuck penning the story of their life? They are stood staring at the equivalent of a blank page just wishing that someone would help by giving them the ideas, support and wisdom they need to write the next page. They don't have the assurance of God's word that all things will work out for good, or that he has plans to prosper them and a great future. They haven't been able to get a sneak preview of the end of their story to give them hope and help them face another day. This is why we need to be prolific writers and keep the chapters flowing. The church should be the equivalent of a spiritual lending library that is open to the world. It should be a place where those who have writers-block can come and read a book that matches their situation in life. Every shelf should be stacked with useful knowledge, insight and hope to help them improve their journey. If we commit to giving our story away our lives will become a valuable resource to those around us.

Growing up I remember my Grandad being an amazing man, so kind and caring. Yet hidden within him was the most incredible story, but it took a great deal of nudging to encourage him to share it. He served in World War Two on the front line and was also involved in Morse Code communications. I had seen pictures of him in his army uniform but couldn't relate to that image of my Grandad.

In Her Shoes

One day I started to ask him questions about it and eventually he gave in and started to talk about his wartime experiences. He told me about the day his tank got hit by enemy fire and his friends died in the explosion. I could sense the discomfort he felt as he relived that painful moment. He described some of the assignments he had been involved in using his Morse Code skills and I was completely fascinated. I could have sat for hours as he opened the book of his life and allowed me to read. I entered his shoes and saw my Grandad in a totally new way. I learned from his life and saw his bravery, strength and courage through him sharing his story. His honesty, openness and vulnerability touched my heart that day and I will always be grateful for it.

My Grandad is no longer with us and I am so glad that I managed to read a few more chapters of his life before he died. Now I can pass those precious pages on to his great-grandchildren and his story will live on. What about you, what stories do you need to pass on? Are you lending them to others or keeping them hidden away?

It's time to blow the dust off the book of your life and put it back in the lending library.

In Her Shoes

We need to revive the art of storytelling once again and share the story of our lives so that people can see God's greatness, his faithfulness and love for the world. Maybe you are thinking, 'Me, tell my story! I don't have anything interesting to say!' That is where you are wrong my friend. Your entire life is a story, and if we can learn from sheep and coins then I'm sure we can learn from you.

We need to realise that everyone's journey is someone else's guidance. Every mistake made is someone else's pain-free piece of wisdom. There are people who desperately need to hear your story because it has the power to breathe hope into their situation, it can illuminate an exit sign and show them the way out when they didn't think there was one. It can restore joy to people who are in a valley of tears. Maybe you need to start making more stops. Instead of rushing past on your journey, slow down, stop and let others board your life, invite them to step into your shoes so that they can walk more easily in their own.

If everyone started using the gift of storytelling in the way God intended, I believe we would see a lot more salvation on the planet. God's goodness would become much more tangible to people and his truth and wisdom would become accessible to many more. It is the job of each of us to connect with others and we all have the tool with which to make this happen; it is the gift of storytelling. So, who could you reach if you started to tell them the story of your life? It's easy to begin, just open up your story at any part and start to share your own 'once upon a time.' Who can you nudge and who can you connect with?

THERE IS A CALL FOR US
TO LEAVE NEVERLAND

FOR BEYOND IT
IS A WORLD
WE MUST REACH

CHAPTER 4

Leaving Neverland

Recently I was at home with my family eating popcorn and watching the Disney movie 'Peter Pan'. I felt God grab my attention as a particular scene played out. It was the one where a young girl, Wendy, is getting ready to go to bed in the nursery. She is playing around with her younger brothers and causing chaos when her father comes in to kiss her goodnight and says, 'Wendy, that's enough. This is your last night in the nursery. Tomorrow it's time to grow up.' He leaves and then the window blows open and in comes Peter Pan. He tells her not to worry about her Father's orders and assures her that she doesn't need to grow up. She can go with him to a special place called Neverland.

As I watched this scene I felt God whisper to my spirit, 'It's time for many of my kids to leave the nursery and grow up.' You may think you have grown-up and might be in

In Her Shoes

your mid-life or older. But it's really not how many years you have been around that counts. The question is, have you really grown up or just grown old? Growing old is inevitable, we only have to look in the mirror and spot our latest wrinkle or grey hair to see that. Certain parts of your body will start to go south, whether you want them to or not! We all grow old but it's a personal choice whether we grow up. Like Wendy in Peter Pan, we can choose whether or not to listen to our Father and grow up, or keep hanging out in Neverland.

I have found that Neverland is a very popular destination for many people. We want to stay in the nursery and often create nursery style churches that keep everyone happy, well-fed and entertained. After all, growing up sounds so boring and is hard work. Therefore we have a tension between what we feel like doing and what we need to do. But no-one will ever be helped by a life that stays in the nursery.

People who have a Peter Pan mentality live in their own version of Neverland. They never follow through on what they say; they never really commit to anything; they never say what they really mean and they never grow up enough to take on the responsibility God requires from them. There are many 'Peter Pans' who entice us to stay in that place of immaturity, but while we are there our lives stay small and our vision and experience is restricted. We need to listen to the call of our Father's voice, to his request for us to grow up because outside the nursery is another world that we must reach. If you want your life and story to impact those around you then growing up isn't optional.

Lessons From A Fugitive

The story of Jonah is a Bible classic that is often taught in Sunday School. We know him as the man who was swallowed by a big fish but there is so much more to it than that. Jonah was someone who understood the importance of growing up and giving his story away. He got to write a book about his life but instead of listing his finest moments he chose to write about his bad attitude and his childish behaviour. I love Jonah for his blatant honesty, he was willing to be real, to invite us into his shoes and let us learn from his life. Jonah was called by God to go to Nineveh and preach to the people there. His outright refusal to go there showed that even though he was a prophet, there were areas of his life that he had

In Her Shoes

never grown-up in. He may have looked like an adult on the outside but there was immaturity in his heart which threatened to derail both his destiny and the future of thousands of Ninevites.

It says in Jonah, *'The word of the Lord came to Jonah son of Amittai: "Go to the great city of Nineveh and preach against it, because its wickedness has come up before me." But Jonah ran away from the Lord and headed for Tarshish' (Jonah 1:1-3)*.

We need to dig a bit deeper to understand what was really going on here. Why didn't Jonah want to go to Nineveh? God hadn't asked him to do something that was outside his capabilities, the task wasn't too difficult for him. The real problem was that he didn't want to help the people there. He had already decided in his heart that they didn't deserve God's mercy or grace to be extended to them because of the sinful lives they were leading. Jonah had judged the people of Nineveh in his heart and his own feelings about the matter became a massive stumbling block to him responding to God's call. The problem that Jonah had was with his heart, it was too small to embrace what God had asked of him and he had some growing to do.

In Her Shoes

It's Not Just About You

At the very start of Jonah's story we discover one of the key reasons why we need to grow. Our lives are not just about us, we are called to reach others. There were one hundred and twenty thousand men, women and children in Nineveh who were lost and unless they repented then they would be destroyed. Their lives depended on Jonah doing what God had asked of him because they needed that second chance that God was offering them.

If like Jonah, you are facing a grow-up moment, then think about the other people whose stories may be intertwined with yours. Think about the people who God is sending to you, think about the impact that your life can have on them. One thing that Jonah forgot to do was to put himself in the shoes of those people, maybe some of them had never heard that there was another way to live. Many of them would have known nothing but the evil ways of Nineveh since the day they were born and they deserved that opportunity to experience God's mercy and grace. It is easy for us to think that Jonah had a terrible attitude, but unless we are careful we can make the same mistake. We need to be people who are always willing to say yes to God

In Her Shoes

and that is why we need to step out of our own comfy shoes and stand in someone else's.

Growing Pains

When our daughter was about three, I heard her screaming one night. I quickly ran to her bedroom and turned the light on to find out what was wrong. It was about three o'clock in the morning and she was crying with her eyes tightly shut. She was sobbing saying, 'My legs, Mummy it's my legs!' She was in agony, and had really bad cramps, so I called my husband. We got hot flannels to soothe her legs and gently massaged them until she managed to get back to sleep. This happened several nights in a row. As concerned first time parents we took her to the Doctor to find out what was causing such distress. To our relief, he told us there was nothing wrong with her, it was just growing pains. Her legs needed to grow and her body was aching as it accommodated that physical need.

As I thought about this in the natural I saw that the same is also true with our spiritual growth. We want to grow and yet we don't want the growing pains, but you can't have one without the other. In fact we need the pains to ensure the growth is genuine and felt. There are many mistakes, lessons, pride issues and attitudes that we have to deal with and unfortunately if there is no pain, there is no gain. For many people that is where they exit the journey. They don't want to suffer self-inflicted growing pains and would rather be a spiritual midget than grow a healthy life. Growing pains are something which we all experience as we embrace change and allow God to work in our life. He is trying to correct and challenge you because he wants you to step into the next chapter of your life. Jonah's story shows us how growing is not always a comfortable experience. Growth stretches you and this can be painful at times as God challenges and changes us, but it is something we cannot do without.

The Wake Up Call

God is committed to helping us grow our lives. He sees the potential that lies within us and wants that to be realised. If we don't respond to him the first time then there may be something else heading in our direction to make us sit up and take notice. For Jonah running away was just the beginning of his self-inflicted troubles.

In Her Shoes

'He went down to Joppa, where he found a ship bound for that port. After paying the fare, he went aboard and sailed for Tarshish to flee from the Lord. The Lord sent a great wind on the sea, and such a violent storm arose that the ship threatened to break up. All the sailors were afraid and each cried out to his own god. And they threw the cargo into the sea to lighten the ship.'

(Jonah 1:3-5)

Sometimes when a storm hits our life our reaction can be like that of the sailors, we cry out to God. But if no amount of praying or rebuking can make it go away then maybe we should stop what we are doing for a moment and think about where it has come from. Maybe it is a wake up call from God because he is trying to get your attention. Not every difficult circumstance is from the enemy and this storm was God's way of stopping Jonah in his tracks. It was caused by Jonah's own disobedience because if he had gone straight to Nineveh he would never have had to face the storm.

We also need to realise that the decisions we make can also have serious implications for those around us. The storm was caused because of Jonah's disobedience and because

In Her Shoes

of his behaviour the lives of everyone on board the ship were in danger. Their future depended on Jonah's ability to grow up and obey the instructions God had given him. In the same way that people needed Jonah to grow up there are also people who need you and I to grow up. This is why God places such importance on our response to growth. He is so committed to your growth that he will orchestrate a storm or other situations just to stop us in our tracks and help guide us back towards his original plan.

Whale Vomit

Devoting yourself to growth is costly, it will mean embracing change on a regular basis. It will involve letting God deal with issues in your heart that are preventing your progress. When Jonah was thrown overboard during the storm and swallowed by the whale this was stage two in his learning curve.

For Jonah the whale became his 'time out', his place of solace and a chance for him to reflect on his life and the choices he had made. From time to time we all need this kind of space in our world. It took three days of being in the whale's stomach before Jonah finally uttered the

In Her Shoes

words God was waiting to hear. He prayed to God saying, *' "But I, with a song of thanksgiving, will sacrifice to you. What I have vowed I will make good. Salvation comes from the Lord." '* (Jonah 2:9)

This showed a change in Jonah's heart, it was grown-up language which showed that he was ready to take responsibility for his life and the situation he found himself in. It can be very easy to vow things to God, but far more difficult to carry out what you have promised. God had to bring Jonah to a fresh place of remembering what his life was really about.

The whale is a place where many stories are formed. Often we want to ignore the whale moments, we would rather just move on and not talk about the fact we had to get in a whale. But the whale was a gift to Jonah's world. It was a place of safety from the raging storm and instead of drowning he spent time searching, and instead of panicking he came to a place of repentance. His story was rewritten in the whale, he got to choose a different ending. Jonah rewrote his commitment to God, he rewrote his decision to obey and I am so thankful it is recorded for us to read because at times we will all experience the whale.

In Her Shoes

Instead of seeing it as punishment we need to learn from Jonah and realise that it could be the making of us and the saving of others. The finale of Jonah's story was Nineveh, and after much soul searching and his decision to grow through the experience the whale spat him out onto dry land. After you arrive at the same conclusion you will also find dry land under your feet.

What's That Smell?

Being thrown up as whale vomit was hardly the most graceful end to his ordeal but there was only one way out. This is a part of the story that we can often skip over, but there is so much more for us to learn from it. First of all this whale vomit was divine. It is very unusual behaviour for a whale to swallow a human and then spit them out at an exact location. This whale was a gift to Jonah not a punishment. It was a place of dealing with some difficult attitudes and wrong thinking but it was also a place of grace covering him. God in his goodness didn't expose Jonah, he hid him under the ocean until he had worked through his challenges.

In Her Shoes

Even more amazing is that whales don't usually vomit and this rare behaviour actually produces something very valuable. You may think that Jonah came out with a disgusting smell from the whale but the opposite is actually true. Jonah came through the experience with an amazing aroma. Whale vomit is actually a substance that is better known as ambergris. This black, gooey mixture turns waxy after being baked in the sun and worn smooth by the action of the sea. Ambergris has a strong, pleasant pine smell and is sought after because it is used in the manufacturing process to make some of the worlds finest smelling perfumes. It's an ingredient in fragrances such as Chanel No.5 and a small piece of whale vomit is worth thousands of pounds.

When Jonah finally arrived in Nineveh, many teach that he arrived stinking of fish and looking dishevelled after his punishing whale experience. I think he arrived humbled as he was reminded of God's grace and all that he was called to do. It says that on the first day he reached Nineveh the people of the city all got down on their knees and repented. I wonder if there was a powerful aroma coming off Jonah's life that he wasn't even aware of from the time he had spent in the whale. The fact is genuine growth is expensive, it is costly for you to embrace it but what comes next will be valuable and it will change the fragrance of your life. You will have a unique aroma because of the price you had to pay and the journey you had to take. It will speak of the depths you have been to with God, of the work he has done in your heart during those difficult times. It is this scent that we can carry to our families, our communities and to wherever he sends us.

Consistent Growth

Sometimes like Jonah we can be faced with defining growth moments, but for much of our lives growth isn't always so obvious. Growing-up is a process, it takes time as we learn new lessons and develop our character and it comes through the choices we make everyday.

I first felt the weight of these choices to grow-up as a teenager. I'd always had a desire to serve God and loved his House. I felt drawn to be around the things of God. I would cry at being left behind when the adults went to meetings. I would even forgo a trip to the movies for a trip with my Dad to church. On one occasion I remember crying because he was going to a meeting without me, so he gave in to my tears and scooped me up in my pink slippers and dressing gown and took me with him. When we arrived I sat in a room full of men discussing finances and issues in the church. I just sat there in my pink slippers not understanding anything they said but still loving every minute of it. I know I was weird!

When I was fourteen, my parents were attending a leadership meeting and I really wanted to go. It was a meeting for adults and I was too young. My parents agreed to smuggle me into the meeting. Considering that I wasn't even supposed to be there, I was totally surprised when the speaker approached my parents saying he had a word for me. He even struggled with it being for me because I was still a young girl. But he knew my parents well so he delivered the word he felt he was carrying over my life. The word was very detailed, about my future, health, husband, children and about a ministry God would give me. He said I would open the Word and teach many people. You have to understand that this was a million miles away from my day to day life. I wasn't even thinking about my future or my marriage, definitely not ministry, and certainly not pregnancy! (Little did I know that years later I would be told that I was infertile and this word would be a ray of light and hope to my soul, but that is another story).

I have been brought up well grounded in the things of God so instead of letting this word scare me or define me I allowed it to be a source of encouragement to me on my journey. It reminded me to trust God and stay open to what was ahead, but I also remember it being a wake-up call for me to grow up. I remember going home that night and lying in bed thinking, 'Thanks! Now what? I'm only fourteen.' So I started to read about Timothy's life. He was a young man with a call from God to fulfil and he had to decide whether or not to grow-up. I read these verses which we often quote, but they came alive to me in a new way.

In 1 Timothy, Paul says, '*Don't let anyone look down on you because you are young, but set an example in your speech, in life, in love, in faith, and in purity. Until I come, devote yourself to the public reading of Scripture, to preaching and to teaching. Do not neglect your gift, which was given you through a prophetic message when the body of elders laid their hands on you. Be diligent in these matters. Give yourself wholly to them, so that everyone may see your progress. Watch your life and doctrine closely. Persevere in them, because if you do, you will save both yourself and your hearers' (1 Timothy 4:12-16).*

The words that jumped out at me were not, *'don't let anyone look down on you because you are young,'* but the next bit that starts with, *'set an example.'* It then continues with a list of instructions to Timothy of what he needed to do so that people wouldn't look down on him. He had to commit to follow through on his part of the workload. Timothy had to grow-up, he was going to have to rule his speech, work on his faith and be an example to others in the way he lived. He was told not to neglect his gift but to devote himself to scripture. In other words Timothy had an amazing gift but now it was time for him to get to work on it. That was a tall order for such a young man, it was a task which required a certain level of maturity. This was his call to leave the nursery.

Paul instructed Timothy in the next verse, *'Do not rebuke an older man harshly, but exhort him as if he were your father. Treat younger men as brothers, older women as mothers, and younger women as sisters, with absolute purity. Give proper recognition to those widows who are really in need' (1 Timothy 5:1-3).*

In Her Shoes

Timothy was going to be required to help many other people from very different walks of life and that's why he had to mature. He was going to have to look after widows and instruct older men so he had to learn to first grow his compassion, knowledge and wisdom so he could connect and walk in their shoes. He needed the ability to empathise with them and step into the shoes of the old, the young, the married and the widows. To fulfil his calling Timothy had to kick-start a growth spurt in his life and embrace all it involved. He had to set an example and devote himself to growth and that is what God also asks of us. I don't know about you but I don't want God to have to send a whale into my world to swallow me because I refuse to grow-up, and I don't want to live a Peter Pan life that is restricted by the four walls of the nursery. I want to keep growing and embracing the challenges that God brings to my life so that I can continue to be useful to God in helping reach others.

There are certain characteristics that mark out a mature life and separate a grown-up from someone who displays childish behaviour. It is important that we learn to identify these and develop them in our own lives so that we can continually measure our growth.

IF THE SHOE FITS
KEEP GROWING

CHAPTER 5

What's Your Shoe Size?

If we want to step into the shoes of others, then it is essential to keep growing. Growth enables you to write new chapters of your story so that you can connect with new listeners. Every time you are stretched and your life expands as you respond to God, it adds a new dimension to your developing story. Nothing is wasted, even your failures can encourage others as much as your success if you learn valuable lessons that can be passed on.

If we want to engage with as many people as possible then we can't afford to restrict our storytelling to one great anecdote which we repeat over and over again. Eventually people will become bored of our repetitious life and we will become just another fairytale in the storybook collection rather than a running commentary of the grace and goodness of God in our life. Individuals and churches alike must decide to keep writing their story. Your growth will ensure new adventures, it will keep you connecting with new travellers and will allow you to step into new shoes. Many have restricted their shoe size because they don't want to face the expense that accompanies growth.

As a parent I sometimes wish my children's feet wouldn't grow so fast. Every time they get their feet measured they have grown again which means buying more shoes. Our spiritual growth is just the same. We have to decide whether we are willing to keep growing and keep paying the cost or squeeze our life into an ill-fitting shoe and stunt our future growth. We all need a way of measuring our shoe size and a commitment to keep growing.

Growth can happen at different rates, sometimes it is slow and at other times you hit a growth spurt and the process speeds up. Maybe you are seeing steady growth right now, or perhaps you can feel your spiritual shoe size increasing at a rapid rate. Either way there are some common markers you can look for which are the signs of a growing life. Let's consider a few of them.

In Her Shoes

Measuring Your Shoe Size

Growth Marker 1: Decisiveness

Children always make decisions by group consensus. If you ask a child what they think they will tell you what all their friends think. They make decisions based on acceptance and being liked. They want to blend in throughout their early years and not stand out. But one of the marks of a grown-up is their willingness to stand up and speak out, even if that means they may have to go it alone.

Recently our daughter and a few other children were being bullied by a young boy called Geoffrey. One night as she was chatting about this I suggested trying to see if we could sort it out. Anyone would have thought that I had said something life-threatening. She was so upset at the thought of breaking rank from some of her friends who were suffering in silence and didn't want to stand out. So I gently explained to her that if we did this, maybe we could also help everyone else, even the naughty boy. Yes, even at five years old we have grown-up decisions to make. The next day we found out more about Geoffrey and discovered that there were some difficult circumstances surrounding his life. We stepped into his shoes and tried to understand why he was behaving in this way. The boy was spoken to by an adult in his world who wanted to help him and since then it has been a lot easier. Our daughter learnt how to handle the situation and many kids have benefited from the decision of one to grow-up.

This struggle to break rank can be true for all of us whether we are five or fifty five. We can let life's circumstances or people bully us into not standing up. We can let insecurity or shyness overshadow who we are, and it's all too easy to end up following someone else's lead instead of growing up ourselves. At some point you have to embrace the pain threshold, whatever that is for you, and make a decision. That day my daughter had to face the fact that doing what she did could have made her life harder. She might have been seen as the tell-tale, but actually the pain was worth the pay off. She still isn't, and will probably never be best friends with this little boy who she was afraid of. The outcome isn't always perfect. In fact I have to laugh because the other day she said, 'Mummy, today was a great day.' When I asked why she simply said, 'I didn't see Geoffrey!'

In Her Shoes

David's Decisiveness

King David is a great example of a teenage boy who chose to grow up and make some decisions of his own. He decided to leave the comfort of minding the sheep and face a giant. He stood separate from his brothers who criticised and jeered him as he went to face Goliath. The courage he showed must have embarrassed them because he showed up their immaturity by leaving the group and breaking rank. He refused to let them hold him back and soon found himself in front of the king of Israel who offered him his armour to wear. Yet again David was faced with making another grown-up decision because now he had King Saul trying to control him, dress him, tell him what to do. David decided to be true to himself. He stood up to the king and politely declined his help because although he didn't know how to wear armour he did know how to use a sling and a stone. David stepped out into the destiny God had for him by refusing to wear the ill-fitting footwear of immaturity and control that others had chosen for him, and we need to do the same. He wrote himself into the history books and got an amazing story that we are still learning valuable lessons from today.

IN HER SHOES

What about the young prophet Elisha? He was faced with the decision of leaving his peers behind to follow Elijah, but they wanted him to stay. When their mentor Elijah announced it was his time to go, Elisha said, 'I'm not leaving your side, I want to be with you in your final moments.' The older prophet told him to leave ten times, but Elisha knew this was a defining moment in his life and nothing could dissuade him. Each time he made that decision to stay by the prophet's side he grew and qualified his life for the responsibility that God had lined up for him.

The other prophets of his day encouraged him to stay back with the group and remain the same shoe size. They wanted him to remain with them on the opposite river bank, yet he knew that if he was to be all God had intended he had to make the decision to step out, cross the river and follow Elijah. In doing so Elisha got a double portion of Elijah's anointing.

Anyone who wants to grow needs to hear the voice of God for themselves and make good decisions from the strength of their convictions. They must keep advancing even when others are holding back and have the confidence to leave the crowd. At the end of the day it is our own responsibility to remove any limitations, indecisiveness and doubt out of our way because no-one else will do it for us.

Older Doesn't Mean Wiser

Growth Marker 2: Accepting 'No'

A clear marker of a growing life can be seen in our reaction to the word 'no!' An immature life always wants its own way, if you want to grow then you need to accept 'no' as a valid answer at times. Nobody likes to hear the word 'no' but it is extremely important. Just think for a moment about how it operates in a child's life. The word 'no' is a lifesaver. You are passing on your wisdom by saying no, 'No, you can't eat chocolate for breakfast. No you can't touch that flame. No you're not leaving school, you're only eleven years old!' We use the word 'no' to protect and grow them. Yet as adults we seem to forget this principle, but being older doesn't always make us wiser. In some cases a 'no' is exactly what we need to hear to save our life and the lives of others. If we can't accept the 'no' then we'll all become obsessed with trying to change a 'no' to a 'yes' and end up chasing things that will keep us small.

In Her Shoes

Tears And Tantrums

I have met sulky adults before. In fact I have been one on several occasions, sulking because it's not fair. It sounds ridiculous but we are all capable of doing it and it's the ultimate behaviour of a child.

In 1 Kings 21, there is the story of a king called Ahab who had the responsibility of being a ruler. He was entrusted with power to rule and help people yet he was a king by name but not by nature. He was immature, selfish and wouldn't take 'no' as a valid answer.

It says, *'Sometime later there was an incident involving a vineyard belonging to Naboth the Jezreelite. The vineyard was in Jezreel, close to the palace of Ahab King of Samaria. Ahab said to Naboth, "Let me have your vineyard to use for a vegetable garden, since it is close to my palace. In exchange I will give you a better vineyard or, if you prefer, I will pay you whatever it is worth." But Naboth replied, "The Lord forbid that I should give you the inheritance of my fathers." So Ahab went home, sullen and angry because Naboth the Jezreelite had said, "I will not give you the inheritance of my fathers." And he lay on his bed sulking and refused to eat'* (1 Kings 21:1-4).

In Her Shoes

Here is a king who had so much and yet had learnt so little. He was given big shoes to wear and yet didn't grow enough to fill them. Ahab seemed to have it all and yet he was the ultimate picture of power without responsibility. This king was sulking over one small vineyard even though he had plenty of money to buy land elsewhere. The problem was he just couldn't handle being told 'no!'

This was when Ahab's wife entered the story. I'm sure she was fed up living with his moody behaviour so she decided to fix the problem herself and cheer up her sulky husband. She had Naboth killed so the king could have the vineyard and his failure to mature and accept the word 'no' caused the death of an innocent man. We must be careful that we do not encourage or condone this kind of behaviour like Ahab's wife did. Someone should have told him to grow up and put a measuring chart against his life to show him the gap caused by his immaturity. All Ahab cared about was his own personal comfort, he lived with his feet firmly planted in his own shoes and showed no regard for others. If he had been willing to grow he would have stepped into Naboth's shoes, had some concern for his situation and accepted the word 'no'.

In Her Shoes

It sounds like extreme behaviour, but this is a picture of how we can end up behaving when we don't get what we want. You didn't get the position on the Worship Team. You didn't get called to preach this week. You didn't get mentioned when the Pastor was thanking everybody for making the food for the event. You got overlooked or your child didn't get a leading role in the Christmas play. Even I had to check my spirit when our son was asked to play a cow in the nativity play! Have you ever been offended when a friend started to spend time with a different group of people instead of you, or thrown a tantrum because you didn't get your own way and said, 'It's not fair!' Meanwhile your good Christian friend is saying, 'That is not right, I'll sort it out for you!' They climb on your bandwagon to help you fight a fight that was never meant to be fought and as a result other people are hurt in the fall-out. It's time to stop the tears and tantrums, because this kind of behaviour is not beneficial for God's people.

When Jesus was on the cross he demonstrated the ultimate grow-up moment when he said, 'Not my will but yours be done.' He didn't want to endure the pain of the cross and just hours earlier he had prayed to his Father asking if this cup could be taken from him. In that final statement he was saying this is not about me and what I want, it's about the big picture. Thank God he did because his act of obedience ensured our salvation. The truth is that Jesus went to the cross because he put himself in your shoes and mine. He decided that you were worth it and surrendered his life, he chose his pain for our gain. Jesus saw your face and mine, he saw our lostness and decided to bridge that gap. Every time you forgo your own feelings and make a grown-up choice it benefits others. That is why 'no' is a word that grows you. It forces you to leave the nursery and start to help others. So if you need help to make the right decisions then put yourself in their shoes. Put yourself in the shoes of the people who will benefit from you taking on the bully or facing Goliath. Put yourself in the shoes of your kids who will benefit from you ending that relationship. Put yourself in the shoes of the people in your community who will be rescued by the ministry you start. If you can see life from their perspective then I guarantee it will spur you on.

In Her Shoes

Want Or Crave?

The truth is growing up isn't easy. Who wants to leave the toys behind and go to school? Who wants to leave university and get a real job? Who wants to leave home and pay a mortgage? Each level requires less selfishness and rather than just seeing growth as something that is thrust on us we need to embrace it and learn to love it. The best thing you can do is develop an appetite for growth. See its beauty, how it can help you help others, see its potential and crave what it will bring. If you ask a pregnant woman if she wants to give birth her answer would be no. But if you ask her if she will give birth, her answer will be yes because the baby is more important to her. A mother's desire for her baby and its well-being is such a powerful force that it can drive her through even the worst of labours. You just keep going for the sake of that child. We need to find a similar drive in our attitude towards growing up in God.

The Bible gives us some clear guidance on how to go about growing. It tells us that we should crave it. 1 Peter says, *'Like newborn babies, crave pure spiritual milk, so that by it you may grow up in your salvation'* (1 Peter 2:2).

In Her Shoes

The word 'crave' means to long for something, to want it greatly and to eagerly desire it. It seems like an unusual word to use to describe how you should feel about growing up. When you crave something your behaviour towards it isn't half-hearted. You actively seek it out because you just can't do without it.

I learnt a lot about what it means to have a craving when I was pregnant. I developed a craving for orange yoghurts and they proved very hard to find. I could find plenty of jaffa yoghurts, or tangerine and banana yoghurts but they weren't the same. They had to be orange. I would say to my husband Steve in the middle of the night, 'Find me an orange yoghurt, I need an orange yoghurt!' And like any sensible man whose wife is heavily pregnant he did his very best to find me one. We often ended up driving around late at night looking for any open shops that might sell them! It was a lot harder than you might think! That is the kind of insatiable desire that we need to have for God and his plans for our life. We need to be at the point where nothing else will do, nothing else can satisfy. We must crave growth so much that we will be prepared to go to any lengths to achieve it. That is the kind of spiritual hunger that will help us grow up. Just having a 'want' for God isn't enough. You need to develop a craving. If you only 'want' to do something for Jesus, then there will come days when your 'want' isn't strong enough to move you forward and you will end up abandoning your good intentions. But the word crave also means to go after and pursue with all that's in you. If you crave to be useful for God and crave to do what God has called you to do, then this will keep you going despite the pain.

There are so many other things that clamour for our time and attention in life that unless we crave God and the growth plan he has for us it's too easy to get distracted and put it off to a later date. We don't need any more late bloomers in the Kingdom of God. We need every person to grow in keeping with the plan God has for their life.

Grown Up Fun

By now you could be reading this thinking 'I'm fed up, I don't want to grow up. It means pain, decisions and selflessness!' So before you make a quick exit and put book down in exchange for a more cheery read, I want to tell you that growing up is so much fun. God has saved the best adventures, the most fun, excitement and exhilaration for grown-ups. Have you ever been to a theme

In Her Shoes

park and seen signs saying that you must be a certain height to go on a ride? These signs are always next to the scariest looking but most thrilling rides. Next to them you also see rows of young kids trying desperately to measure up. They are stood on their tiptoes, or restyling their hair into a mohawk, desperately hoping to add those three missing inches that disqualifies them. Alternatively you see reluctant parents who only wish they could get out of the ride by being a lot shorter.

We recently went to a theme park and one of our kids decided that she wanted to ride the log flume. We didn't believe her at first because it had a huge dip and looked far too scary for a five year old, but she persisted. I was definitely not going on the ride, so I rested secure in the fact that there would be a measuring bar and she would be nowhere near tall enough. You can imagine my horror when she stood next to the pole and was exactly the right height to go on it. We ended up going on the log flume and I was sure we would have tears, either hers or mine. But it was only shrieks of sheer delight that came out as we had fun with every twist, turn and eventual drop.

In Her Shoes

God has placed spiritual measuring bars to protect you, the rider, and those on board from any immature passengers taking on more than they can handle. The fact is that the rides with measuring bars are the most fun and you need to grow up to experience them for yourself. Too many Christians live their life on the spiritual equivalent of the teacup ride going round and round to music that puts you to sleep. They see the same scenery, the same faces, sing the same songs and face the same needs day in, day out. Teacup Christians never walk in anyone else's shoes or take a risk by reaching out to someone new who is outside their mundane merry-go-round life. Now surely you can't call that fun!

Just think about the guys in Daniel's day. They all went along with the king when he commanded them to disobey and forsake their beliefs. They let their fear and immaturity keep them small, but Daniel made a decision to grow and stand out from the crowd. He said 'No, I refuse to do that!' His friends chose to blend in but he chose to stand out and by doing so he measured up for the ride of his life. He spent a night in the lions den! His grown-up decision increased his spiritual height so while they were getting bored on the teacups, he used a lion for

In Her Shoes

a pillow. That was one great story he had to tell them the next day! I'd certainly rather have a story to tell about trying to walk on water than about sitting in the boat, or about risking my life and managing to save thousands of people rather than having to admit being too afraid to try.

Maybe you are too used to a 'teacup ride existence' and didn't realise that you can choose to get off them and onto something more exciting. I want to urge you to get your measuring stick out and start checking your growth on a regular basis. Make growth a priority in your life and aim to keep increasing your spiritual shoe size. Decide to stand up, get a craving for growth and qualify your life for some bigger rides so that you can help more people. Go on, I dare you!

SO MUCH CHOICE
SO LITTLE TIME!

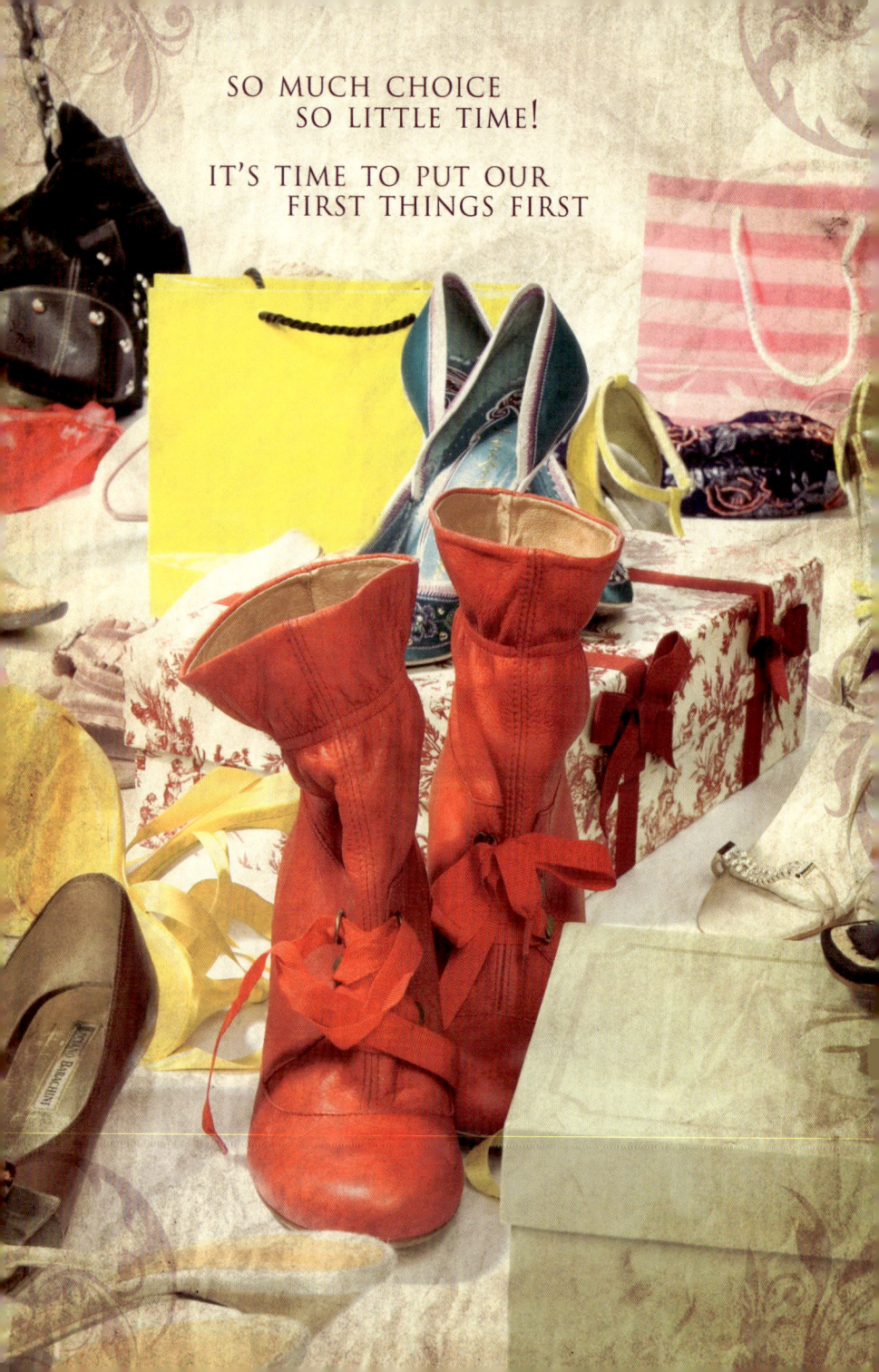

IT'S TIME TO PUT OUR
FIRST THINGS FIRST

CHAPTER 6

First Things First

Committing to walk in the shoes of others will not only challenge you to grow, but it will also challenge how you prioritise your life. When the disciples were first called to follow Jesus their lives changed in an instant. In order to respond they had to be willing to reprioritise their lives. Jesus didn't give them any time to think and pray about following him. He didn't say, 'Think about it for a while and talk to your family about whether this is the right time for you!' Jesus just kept on moving as he called for them to follow, and in that split second they decided to radically reshape their world.

Are you ready to respond to the 'follow me' call of God on your life? We need to examine our lives and look at how much time we actually allow for God to use us to fulfil his agenda. We can think that our heart is open to interruptions, until like Jonah we hear the call to go to

In Her Shoes

Nineveh, a place we hadn't even planned on visiting. It's these moments that make us realise our priorities don't match up with God's. I've discovered that the call to follow Jesus is highly inconvenient, and stepping into the shoes of others will often require you to reschedule your life.

The Inconvenient Call

I love how the disciples didn't think twice about following Jesus, they just left what they were doing and went with him. I wonder what our response would have been. Would we have stopped what we were doing immediately, or would we have gone back to Jesus with a long list of tasks we had to do before we could go? Can you imagine if Peter had said, 'Yes I'll follow you, but first I need to find someone else to run my fishing business, plus I have a weeks holiday planned next month so I will need a week off!' Sometimes this can be how we answer God's call on our lives. We say 'Yes but,' and then make our response conditional. We run through our other priorities before telling God that our own agenda is more important to us than his.

Don't get me wrong, I know how busy life can be and I am not suggesting that what you need to do isn't important.

In Her Shoes

But we still need to be careful that we don't leave the phone line of our life off the hook, sending God the 'busy' signal. I don't want to end up spending each day trying to race through a long list of things that I need to do only to discover that they were not even on God's list. Our time is stretched in many directions with work, marriage, raising a family, friendships, church and other commitments. There are only twenty four hours in a day and many times that just doesn't seem enough! God has placed us in a time-space world and he understands all the demands this brings. But he also expects that we will obey his voice and make room for his agenda. It says in Matthew, *'Seek first his kingdom and his righteousness, and all these things will be given to you as well' (Matthew 6:33)*. This verse gives us a clue to how God sees this working. If you will prioritise him then he will prioritise you. It sounds like a good deal to me!

We must become far more deliberate about our priorities because they act like a rudder and steer our lives in a particular direction. Your choice of priorities are not neutral, they will determine where you end up, who you reach and what you achieve. Perhaps right now you feel you are sailing in the wrong direction, or maybe it is a

In Her Shoes

while since you checked where you were heading. It says in 1 Corinthians, ' *"Everything is permissible" - but not everything is beneficial. "Everything is permissible" - but not everything is constructive. Nobody should seek his own good, but the good of others"* (1 Corinthians 10:23). We have to decide whether we are living a permissible life or a constructive life. God can't determine this for us, it is something that we need to determine.

Think of your life as if it were a car. Your time and energy are the fuel you fill your vehicle with to keep it moving and the tank only holds a limited supply. We only have a certain amount of fuel available to us every day and we can waste it on things that are permissible, or use it for those that are beneficial. You can use it on your own good or the good of others.

When you operate in the realm of what is permissible rather than what is constructive you will use a lot of energy and often gain very little. I remember when my parents moved home years ago into an old Victorian house. My Mum wanted to restore some of the house's original features and she spent hours stripping off thick paint to restore the beautiful wooden beams in one of the bedrooms. My parents had some young people helping them decorate and they left them briefly while they went to run a few errands. On their return they were greeted by an over enthusiastic helper who had got carried away while he was painting the ceiling. He had thought he was helping by painting the beams as well. I watched my Mum as she tried to contain her frustration as many days of painstaking work stripping the paint that had been wiped out. Although this young man had plenty of energy and a heart to serve, he had wasted a whole day's effort on something that wasn't constructive or even needed. How many times is that a picture of our day, week or even our year?

A Prioritised Life

When Jesus hung on the cross he could say 'it is finished' with all his strength because every day and hour of his life had been carefully ordered. There was nothing left undone, he didn't miss anyone out he was supposed to help and he never allowed his schedule to be hijacked by the personal or religious agendas of others. He didn't say 'it is almost finished?' He wasn't hanging there with regret at the people and opportunities he didn't have time to get to. Jesus knew when to say 'yes' to people and when to say 'no'. If he had tried to keep everyone happy the sick wouldn't have been healed and the disciples wouldn't have been trained. Things that should have been his main focus would just have become another task on a very long list.

If we also want to fulfil everything God has got for us then we must prioritise and make room for his agenda of serving and reaching others.

First Things First

It says in Proverbs, *"Put first things first, prepare your work outside and get it ready for yourself in the field. After that build your house and then establish a home" (Proverbs 24:27 Amplified Bible).* If we want to fulfil our potential then we need to know what our first things are. Your first things are whatever is most important to you. They are what you feel you were put on the planet for, they are what you are passionate about. Your first things are what keep you up at night and they are the things that your life would not be the same without. A prioritised life helps put your first things first.

In Her Shoes

My brother-in-law loves music, it is one of his first things. He is passionate about it so he makes sure it is always part of his day. That doesn't mean that all he ever does is listen to music, but it has to be in his day somewhere so he keeps that first thing first amongst the many other things he has to do. You and I need to know what our first things are and start giving them the attention they deserve if we want to grow and make the most of every opportunity God sends us. Jesus knew what his first things were, one of them was training his team and leaving capable leaders behind who could fulfil all God had for them. His time was limited so he prioritised twelve guys over the crowd and over his family and friends.

In Revelation, the church at Ephesus had many hardworking people but they got their priorities out of order. God rebuked them saying, *'Yet I hold this against you: You have forsaken your first love. Remember the height from which you have fallen! Repent and do the things you did at first' (Revelation 2:4-5)*. I have met many Christians who have made this same mistake, good people who have forsaken their first love. They have forgotten to prioritise what God asked of their life and all their doing is not benefiting anyone. What are your first things, do you

In Her Shoes

even know? Are your first things third or even last on your list? Maybe it's time to reprioritise.

First Or Last?

Moses was someone who discovered this the hard way. Instead of concentrating on his first things by spending time with God and hearing his direction for the people of Israel, he allowed himself to be sidetracked into acting as a judge for the people. All three million of them would bring their quarrels and grumbles to him and he would tell them how to sort out their disputes in accordance with God's law. This was no small task, and he would sit from morning until night as they queued up to see him.

It says in Exodus, *'The next day Moses took his seat to serve as judge for the people, and they stood round him from morning till evening. When his father-in-law saw all Moses was doing for the people, he said, "What is this you are doing for the people? Why do you sit alone as judge while all these people stand around you from morning till evening?" Moses answered him, "Because the people come to me to seek God's will. Whenever they have a dispute, it is brought to me, and I decide between the parties and inform them of God's decrees and laws."*

In Her Shoes

Moses' father-in-law replied, "What you are doing is not good. You and these people who come to you will only wear yourselves out. The work is too heavy for you, you cannot handle it alone" ' (Exodus 18:13-18).

Moses allowed something that should never have been his top priority to take up all his time. On the surface this could appear to be a valid use of his day because he was helping the people God had given him to lead. But it was wearing him out and now his family were suffering too. He was so caught up in what he was doing that it took a visit from his father-in-law, Jethro, to point out that spending every day sorting out a never-ending list of complaints was not benefiting anyone. Jethro encouraged him to re-order his world and suggested that Moses should empower others to help sort out the people's disagreements. This meant that Moses could put his first things first by using the fuel of his life for the one thing he was called to do, lead the people.

It is often in times of growth that our priorities are placed under pressure. When thousands of people were being added to the early church the apostles felt the strain. A problem was brought to their attention from the Grecian

IN HER SHOES

Jews who complained that their widows were being left out when food was being distributed.

It says in Acts, *'In those days when the number of disciples was increasing, the Grecian Jews among them complained against the Hebraic Jews because their widows were being overlooked in the daily distribution of food. So the Twelve gathered all the disciples together and said, "It would not be right for us to neglect the ministry of the word of God in order to wait on tables. Brothers, choose seven men from among you who are known to be full of the spirit and wisdom. We will turn this responsibility over to them and will give our attention to prayer and to the ministry of the word"' (Acts 6:1-4).*

This was a valid concern and a matter that needed resolving but the apostles' response was different to that of Moses. They took the issue, measured it against their first things and resisted the urge to drop what they were doing in order to sort it out themselves. It would have been permissible for the disciples to start dishing out the food to the widows but it would not have been a constructive or beneficial solution. They knew what their first things were. They were called to preach the good news, establish the church and see many saved, so they delegated the task to other highly capable members of their team. Many people benefited from their wise decision, the men who were appointed to serve were given an opportunity to grow and the church continued to increase in number.

Who are you most like? Do you order your priorities like Moses or the apostles? Moses let the demands of life reshuffle his priorities and his first thing ended up last. But when faced with similar demands the apostles answered from the conviction of their priorities and refused to be distracted.

Wrong Time, Wrong Place

In Ecclesiastes there is a verse which can help us understand how we can start to put things in the right order for our lives. It says, *'There is a time for everything, and a season for every activity under heaven' (Ecclesiastes 3:1).* The key to prioritising your life isn't trying to do everything at once but by being sensitive to the season your life is in. In the natural world there is an appropriate behaviour that goes with every season. You wouldn't try to harvest a crop before you have planted it, and you wouldn't wear a winter coat on a hot summer day. It works

In Her Shoes

the same spiritually. We need to make sure that our actions are appropriate for the season we find ourselves in.

King David was a great leader. He knew what his first things were but one day he didn't match his priorities up correctly to the time he was in. It says in 1 Samuel, *'In the spring, at the time when kings go off to war, David sent Joab out with the king's men and the whole Israelite army. They destroyed the Ammonites and besieged Rabbah. But David remained in Jerusalem. One evening David got up from his bed and walked around on the roof of the palace. From the roof he saw a woman bathing. The woman was very beautiful, and David sent someone to find out about her. The man said, "Isn't this Bathsheba, the daughter of Eliam and the wife of Uriah the Hittite?" Then David sent messengers to get her. She came to him, and he slept with her. (She had purified herself from her uncleanness.) Then she went back home. The woman conceived and sent word to David, saying, "I am pregnant."'*

(2 Samuel 11:1-5)

In Her Shoes

David should never have been in Jerusalem. It was the time for kings to be at war but he chose to stay at home. He should have been mindful of his troops, put himself in their shoes, and realised that they needed him with them on the frontline leading the charge. By placing his own needs first David left the door open for wrong priorities to take his time. He had nothing of purpose to do and the sight of a beautiful woman bathing soon attracted his attention. After David fell morally with Bathsheba his priorities changed again and he now carefully ordered his life around his mistake in an attempt to cover his tracks. He called her husband, Uriah, home from the battle hoping that he would sleep with his wife so that her adulterous affair with the king would not be uncovered.

'When David was told, "Uriah did not go home," he asked him, "Haven't you just come from a distance? Why didn't you go home?" Uriah said to David, "The ark and Israel and Judah are staying in tents, and my master Joab and my lord's men are camped in the open fields. How could I go to my house to eat and drink and lie with my wife? As surely as you live, I will not do such a thing!"'

(2 Samuel 11:10-11)

In Her Shoes

David's plan didn't work because Uriah understood which season he was in. It was a time for war and even though he was surrounded by the comforts of home his heart and allegiance was to his fellow soldiers on the battlefield. He walked in their shoes and this guided his priorities. Uriah refused to place his own needs first and decided he would rather sleep on the doorstep than be with his wife. As a result of David's wrong priorities two innocent lives were lost. If he had put himself in the shoes of his men he would have been fighting alongside them that day. Instead he ended up hurting others and sinning against God.

So before we move on let me ask, what are your priorities? If you don't know the answer then try writing them down. Don't let things which should be a priority slip down your list and be neglected. What are your first things? Which relationships and friendships do you need to invest in; what activities or areas of ministry should you be giving yourself to; and whose shoes should you be stepping into?

When we have our priorities in the right order it becomes easier for us to make the right decision, it helps us clarify whether we need to respond with a 'yes' or a 'no!' God is asking us to make room for him in our lives. He shouldn't be number ten on our list of things to do. He wants us to

In Her Shoes

re-order our day so that we can step into the shoes of the people he needs us to reach. We can't do everything but it's our willingness to put God's agenda first that matters.

God needs a people who will make him their first love, who will prioritise others over their own wants and desires. He is looking for a church whose first things are his first things. When we align our priorities with God's we will find we are constantly making time to step into the shoes of others and will be amazed at the difference our lives can make.

BEAUTIFUL READER
YOU WILL BE AMAZED
AT WHAT YOU CAN DO

CHAPTER 7

What Can You Do?

Stepping into the shoes of others will not only cause you to reprioritise your world, it will also challenge you to enlarge your heart and life.

There's a well known verse in Isaiah which says, *'Enlarge the place of your tent stretch your tent curtains wide, do not hold back lengthen your cords, strengthen your stakes' (Isaiah 54:2).* Enlargement is always for a purpose. You make a house bigger to accommodate more people and you get a bigger garage so you can fit more stuff in it and you increase your territory so that more people can dwell there. God isn't interested in big things for the sake of it, but because of what it represents. Enlargement creates room for more people to be reached and included.

In Her Shoes

Enlarging your life works the same spiritually as it does in the natural. When you expand physically you soon discover that you don't fit so well into clothes that suited you before. You struggle to make the buttons meet on those trousers that fitted perfectly a few weeks ago. As a mother of two young children I face this growth challenge regularly. It seems that they can outgrow their clothes within weeks. I have discovered a clever invention to help kid's clothing last for longer. It's an adjustable waist-band that can be let out as they expand. We need to fit one of these waistbands to our life if we want to accommodate the growth God has for us. I have seen too many Christians sitting in tight fitting pants saying, 'I have no more room to enlarge my life. I can't reach out to anyone else because I am too stretched.' But maybe there is more in you than you realise. Your heart can expand and your circle of love can increase, you just need to get some more elasticity fitted.

I want to take a look at the lives of two extraordinary women who decided to respond to the challenge of enlarging their lives. On the outside they didn't look extraordinary and they were from very different backgrounds, one was a prostitute, the other a housewife.

In Her Shoes

But what made them special was their willingness to make room for God. They could have offered many excuses as to why it was inconvenient; their lives were complicated and busy with other priorities but they still chose to take up the challenge. These women enlarged their lives and embraced what God was asking of them despite what it would cost them personally.

The Prostitute

Joshua 2 tells us the story of Rahab. She was a prostitute in the city of Jericho and many people despised her for it. I am so glad that the Bible tells us the context of her story because it shows us how no-one can disqualify themselves from being used by God. She wasn't proud of having to sell her body to make ends meet but she was trapped in this lifestyle. Rahab was a broken and abused woman with a family to support. She was judged by her community and used by many of the men who were part of that same judgemental group. Rahab may have been the last person you would have asked for help, but God sees what others don't. He walked in her shoes and saw that there was far more to her than others acknowledged. Although she probably felt worthless and insignificant, God knew her heart had the capacity to expand, and one night he sent

In Her Shoes

two spies to her home to ask, 'Can you help, can you enlarge your life for me?'

It says in Joshua 2, *'Then Joshua son of Nun secretly sent two spies from Shittim. "Go, look over the land," he said, "especially Jericho." So they went and entered the house of a prostitute named Rahab and stayed there. The king of Jericho was told, "Look! Some of the Israelites have come here tonight to spy out the land." So the king of Jericho sent this message to Rahab: "Bring out the men who came to you and entered your house, because they have come to spy out the whole land." But the woman had taken the two men and hidden them. She said, "Yes, the men came to me, but I did not know where they had come from. At dusk, when it was time to close the city gate, the men left. I don't know which way they went. Go after them quickly. You may catch up with them." (But she had taken them up to the roof and hidden them under the stalks of flax she had laid out on the roof.) So the men set out in pursuit of the spies on the road that leads to the fords of the Jordan, and as soon as the pursuers had gone out, the gate was shut.'*

(Joshua 2: 1-7)

In Her Shoes

Scarlet Cords

What the spies asked of Rahab meant great personal risk. She had to hide them from the king and put her own life in danger in order to save them. Rahab wasn't mindful of her own safety but stepped into the shoes of others and spoke up for them. In return for her help she asked the spies to look at her life and step into her shoes by saving those precious to her.

She said, *'Now then, please swear to me by the Lord that you will show kindness to my family, because I have shown kindness to you. Give me a sure sign that you will spare the lives of my father and mother, my brothers and sisters, and all who belong to them, and that you will save us from death. Our lives for your lives!" the men assured her. "If you don't tell what we are doing, we will treat you kindly and faithfully when the Lord gives us the land." So she let them down by a rope through the window, for the house she lived in was part of the city wall.'*

(Joshua 2: 12-15)

In Her Shoes

Joshua's men made an oath with Rahab that day and promised not to harm her family. They told her to tie a scarlet cord in the window of her house as a sign of the agreement they had made. Her selfless act of expanding her life and making room created a door of opportunity that others could walk through to safety. I believe that God is looking for that scarlet cord on our lives, one that says we are willing to make the stretch, to step out and take the risk so that others can find their freedom.

Rahab could have hidden the men in exchange for her own gain. She could have asked them to pay her for the provision of a safe house, or requested a reward that would benefit her own needs. Many people are happy to take a risk if it creates a door of opportunity for themselves but are not interested in the risk if it is a call to hold the door open for others. I think the favour of God is with those who take the risk, go through the door and then hold it open for the people behind them. If your main motivation for responding is your own gain then forget it. But if you are driven by a desire to help others then God will honour you just like he honoured Rahab. She went to live among the Israelites and ended up in a place far removed from her previous life as a prostitute. God didn't just make room for her in terms of where she lived, he made her life count in a way she could never have imagined. Rahab is listed in the lineage of Christ and it happened as a result of her willingness to enlarge.

What Can You Do?

Enlarging our life is not as difficult as it may sound. Often God is not looking for us to perform some miraculous feat. He didn't expect Rahab to defend her family against Joshua's army or ask her to hide an entire battalion in her house because that was outside her capacity. He just wanted her to do what she could and give two spies a place of safety. In order to enlarge we must start with, 'What can I do?' It's a simple question but often people fail to act because they think they can't do much. Our tendency is to answer this question by saying what we can't do rather than focusing what we can do. But when we do what we can God steps in and does what we can't.

The Housewife

Abigail was a housewife, and her life revolved around running her household. Her life was far from perfect and it didn't help that she was married to a stingy businessman called Nabal. The Bible says, *'She was an*

In Her Shoes

intelligent and beautiful woman, but her husband, a Calebite, was surly and mean in his dealings' (1 Samuel 25:3). His name meant 'fool' and her name meant, 'the joy of her father'. They were far from a perfect match and she could easily have let this relationship keep her small.

When we join the story, David had been camping in the desert with six hundred of his warriors when they approached Nabal to ask for some food and vital supplies. Nabal was wealthy, he certainly wasn't short of a goat or two but generosity wasn't his strong point. His heart was small, he was unwilling to make room for anyone else's needs and refused to step into David's shoes and help him. When the news of what had happened reached David he set off with four hundred of his men to find Nabal and kill him.

This moment of crisis was when the call came for Abigail to make the stretch, to enlarge her heart and step out from under the influence of her stingy husband.

'One of the servants told Nabal's wife Abigail: "David sent messengers from the desert to give our master his greetings, but he hurled insults at them. Yet these men were very good to us. They did not ill-treat us, and the

In Her Shoes

whole time we were out in the fields near them nothing went missing. Night and day they were a wall around us all the time we were herding our sheep near them. Now think it over and see what you can do, because disaster is hanging over our master and his whole household. He is such a wicked man that no-one can talk to him." '

(1 Samuel 25:14 – 17)

The servant didn't request anything outside her abilities, he just said, 'Now think it over and see what you can do.' Abigail took the question at face value and didn't over complicate it. Maybe she even laughed at the thought of how little she had to offer. She couldn't fight David's men or plan a military strategy, but like many of us she could do something and that is all God is after.

So Abigail's response in the face of an advancing army was to do what she could do, and that was to make cakes. What she knew how to do was feed hungry people, so she did it. It's a hilarious picture; four hundred armed men were intercepted by Abigail on a donkey with her giant picnic of bread, cakes and mutton. By doing what she could and making a few sandwiches Abigail enlarged her world, she put herself in David's shoes. She knew he had been offended and that his men were hungry so she said 'sorry', a word Nabal never used, and fed them. By doing so her simple picnic and an apology were enough to divert disaster and death from her household.

Can-Do Living

So what can you do to enlarge your life? It may seem small and it may appear insignificant at the time but if it is what you can do then do it. God is looking for people with a 'can-do' attitude who are willing to take the risk and stretch their lives. He is just asking us to stretch and do what we can and he will put his favour on our obedience. If you don't want to miss the enlargement opportunities that are heading your way then 'what can I do?' needs to become the first question on your lips.

I know that as a Leadership Team here at the Abundant Life Church in Bradford we are determined to build a church that has a can-do attitude which is motivated by a concern for others. We like to ask the question 'what can we do?' and keep making room for more people.

In Her Shoes

Recently there were some terrible floods in the UK. Entire communities were affected with thousands of people having to evacuate their homes which were badly damaged by the water. One of the worse affected areas was about forty miles away from our church near a town called Doncaster. We felt God speak to our heart saying 'See what you can do.' He was wanting more from us than simply praying about it, we needed to take action. We got a plan together and like Abigail began to stockpile some provisions. We made food hampers and some volunteers from our Community Action Teams took them to a community centre where many people were camping out after being made homeless by the floods. Our team went back to support people and befriend them. We organised transport to bring people to church for a barbecue. People from that community got saved through the little that we could do and God used a difficult circumstance for his good because of it. When you do what you can, God uses it. He can reach many people through your willingness to enlarge.

Many of us pray for God to knock on the door of our lives like that but we have to be ready for what comes next. The risk, the unknown, the inconvenience and the disruption that answering the door often brings to our world. One of the most famous stories of people who failed to make room was probably the inn-keepers of Bethlehem. One by one they shut the door in the face of Joseph and Mary who was heavily pregnant. Not one of them was willing to make room so they missed out on being part of history. They missed out on the birth of the Saviour, they missed out on the visit of the three kings, the shepherds and the angels. I can imagine that the whole town was buzzing with excitement the day after Jesus was born. Everyone was talking about what had happened. Meanwhile I am sure that several inn-keepers were kicking themselves for not finding room that night and for not being willing to feel the stretch and embrace the inconvenience. I don't know about you but I don't want God to have to go and knock at the door of someone else's life because I won't make room.

So let me ask, what can you do? Who can you impact, how much can you enlarge your heart for the sake of others? Who can you influence in your community and whose shoes can you step into? Maybe you want to enlarge your heart for others but you don't know where to start. Maybe your stretch is to have lunch with a work colleague who is stressed out and would appreciate someone to talk to. Maybe you can't go to Africa but you could sponsor a child there. Maybe you don't know how to reach a young teenage girl struggling with abuse, but you can partner with a ministry that can. I guarantee that there is more stretch in you, there are others you can reach. It's time for you to look at your life through different eyes and start to see what you can do!

Beautiful reader, you are able to do so much more. With God's guidance you can reprioritise and make room for him to use you. The question is are you willing to shift your focus and start looking to see what you can do? Don't be embarrassed if all you can do is offer your cakes, your room or your time. Give what you have and let it be your way of opening a new door and always be willing to hold it open for others. God loves it when we respond in this way and start putting our faith into action. This is when we will really start to see amazing things happen through our lives.

THERE IS JOY
AND ADVENTURE
AWAITING A LIFE THAT
DARES TO STEP OUT

CHAPTER 8

Stepping Out

As you have read this book I pray it has encouraged you to step out, inspired you to enlarge your world and challenged you to include some more people. The fact is that we live in a time when so much need surrounds us, and as we have answers there is no time to lose. Yet often our good intentions are not enough to make us spring into action. It never ceases to amaze me how we can sing songs that declare our willingness to reach out, 'amen' messages that call us to be mobilised and read books that encourage us to make a difference, yet we still struggle to respond. We need to marry up our desire to help with a renewed determination to follow through and fulfil what God is asking of us. Once we align our heart with our conviction to do something we will be moved to find an outward expression of our good intentions.

In Her Shoes

In this chapter I want to talk about what comes next. What happens when you know you need to step out, enlarge and grow? It's a time when you can feel the fear of the unknown and the risk of moving forward.

The Bible records the story of three people who were faced with this challenge when they were called by God to be part of something incredible. Their names were Zechariah, Elizabeth and Mary, and they were chosen to play a strategic part in history. First in Luke 1, we read how God sent an angel to Zechariah and Elizabeth to ask them if they would enlarge their world. He asked them to carry the baby John, one who would impact a generation and prepare the way for Jesus. Then we see how a young teenage girl called Mary was asked to reprioritise her life and carry Jesus. This wasn't convenient for any of them and it certainly wasn't what they were expecting!

You would think that they would all be very excited at these opportunities and eager to be part of such history making events, but each of them responded very differently. Maybe your heart is stirred to reach out and you can identify with how they reacted when God asked them to stretch their lives. Let's take a look at how they responded.

In Her Shoes

In Zechariah's Shoes

Zechariah and Elizabeth were God fearing people. Zechariah was a priest and a highly respected man of God. It says, *'Both of them were upright in the sight of God, observing all the Lord's commandments and regulations blamelessly' (Luke 1:6).* On this particular occasion it was Zechariah's turn to go into the temple and present the people's sacrifices and prayers. As he was going about his duties God interrupted his day.

'Then an angel of the Lord appeared to him, standing at the right side of the altar of incense. When Zechariah saw him he was startled and gripped with fear. But the angel said to him, 'Do not be afraid, Zechariah; your prayer has been heard. Your wife Elizabeth will bear you a son, and you are to give him the name John. He will be a joy and delight to you, and many will rejoice because of his birth, for he will be great in the sight of the Lord."'

(Luke 1:11-15)

After many years of believing with Elizabeth for a child, Zechariah should have been thrilled with this news. It was an answer to his prayers because they were finally going to have the child they had longed for. The angel went on to explain how this special baby would be a prophet, that he would impact the lives of many people and turn the hearts of the next generation towards God. What more could they have asked for? Their prayers had been answered and they had been chosen to play a part in history. But as Zechariah listened to the angel his mind couldn't keep up. He began to think about how old he was and how inconvenient this was. He wasn't ready to receive the enlargement he had prayed for and was too settled in his comfortable life to make the stretch it required.

We can often respond in this way and I have seen it happen many times. I have been in meetings where people have prayed for revival, but when the lost came they complained about the inconvenience it caused. I have seen people pray for God to increase their ministry and then complain about the work it required. Zechariah had one of those moments when he saw the expensive price tag that was attached to what he had prayed for.

Remember that Zechariah was not a bad guy and he didn't want to disobey God but he let his heart grow small. He stopped enlarging his life and settled for a size he felt comfortable with. Although he didn't realise it, his priorities no longer matched up to those that God had for him. Zechariah wasn't willing to be inconvenienced, and maybe that is where you find yourself. Perhaps God is asking you to stretch too far!

The Silent Treatment

'Zechariah asked the angel, "How can I be sure of this? I am an old man and my wife is well on in years." The angel answered, "I am Gabriel. I stand in the presence of God, and I have been sent to speak to you and to tell you this good news. And now you will be silent and not able to speak until the day this happens, because you did not believe my words, which will come true at the proper time"' (Luke 1:18-20).

What happened next is a lesson for us all. God is so concerned that his purposes are not aborted that he will take action to protect his plans. In the midst of Zechariah's questions and doubt God silenced him, he didn't want his negativity influencing others. This miracle birth didn't just involve Zechariah, his wife was going to have to carry the child. Can you imagine if Zechariah had gone home that night and started to express his nagging doubts

In Her Shoes

saying, 'Do you really think this is wise Elizabeth, how are we going to cope? We are too old and we don't know how to raise a child!' Be careful that you don't act like Zechariah when God asks you to step into the shoes of others by making the same kind of statements. If we focus on our questions and doubts then we can take a God given opportunity and turn it into a stumbling block. If you can't say something constructive then maybe you should keep your lips tightly shut. I have had to learn that sometimes silence is the best gift that we can give to those in our world.

I remember when my husband decided that he wanted to build a half-pipe skate ramp for our youth conference and have skateboarders on stage during the worship. He shared the idea with me one night when I was cooking dinner and my response was, 'That's crazy, someone will break their legs!' Thankfully he didn't listen to me and went on to make his idea happen regardless. I remember watching the skaters on the opening night of the conference and it was awesome. The kids loved it, other skaters came to see it and some of them gave their lives to Christ. I'm so glad that he didn't listen to my 'Zechariah confession'. I have learnt that sometimes I do not have faith for the same things my husband does and vice versa. At those times I have learnt to stay silent and let my faith go to school and grow rather than voice my doubts and risk aborting the God idea he is carrying.

Maybe God is prompting you to step out, but you are full of questions and doubt? It's not wrong to have questions but why don't you try silencing them and trusting God. Don't jeopardise the baby, don't put your lack of faith in someone else's way. Zechariah was struck dumb until he came to a place of faith. Maybe you are pregnant with ideas but are surrounded by Zechariahs. Don't let their doubt determine what you do next. Love Zechariah but don't let go of what God has told you to carry.

Zechariah was there to see John's birth. At the sight of his infant son his confession finally lined up with where God needed it to be and his tongue was loosened. John became the best thing that could have happened to Zechariah. His silence wasn't permanent but it was necessary for a season. It meant that John arrived safe and well, and for the sake of what God wants to do sometimes it's worth saying nothing.

In Her Shoes

In Elizabeth's Shoes

Elizabeth didn't receive a visit from an angel. She was notified about her miracle baby by her husband who came out of the temple white with fear. He was murmuring, unable to speak and making crazy gestures as he tried to explain the angelic encounter that had taken place. It says in Luke, *'Meanwhile the people were waiting for Zechariah and wondering why he stayed so long in the temple. When he came out, he could not speak to them. They realised he had seen a vision in the temple, for he kept making signs but remained unable to speak.'*

(Luke 1:21-22)

Imagine the scene, your husband who is performing his priestly duties suddenly runs out of the temple, mute and playing charades! Elizabeth had a lot to take in, she was going to have a baby and her husband was not able to support her as he usually did. But Elizabeth knew this was God and was ready for the stretch. She had been praying for an opportunity like this to invade her world for many years.

In Her Shoes

Incubation

During her pregnancy Elizabeth took some time out to prepare her heart for John's arrival. She created a space in her world away from the prying eyes and interfering voices while she incubated this gift that God had given her to carry. It says that Elizabeth, *'...went off by herself for five months relishing her pregnancy,' (Luke 1:24, The Message)*. This seems like a strange way to behave. You would have thought it was a time to get as much help as possible because this was going to be a big adjustment for a woman of her age. I can imagine that the sight of an old but heavily pregnant woman walking through the town would have raised quite a few eyebrows. The local gossips would have gone to town talking about this strange phenomenon, and this is why Elizabeth needed to keep herself separate. This was her stretch not anyone else's. Many people around her life would not understand what was going on, so she focused on what God had asked her to do.

Have you ever had an occasion in your life when you have felt a sense of separation because of what you were carrying? Well don't worry because you are in good

In Her Shoes

company. Sometimes I have been excited about a new idea, but I spoke about it prematurely to others who didn't feel the same way and they felt it was their duty to try to talk me out of it. They were good people and when I look back I can see that it was because they were just not in my shoes. When we face similar situations we need to respond like Elizabeth did. If you remind yourself of all the people that this idea will end up blessing I can guarantee that this will spur you on!

I am sure there were times when Elizabeth felt that she needed more support. Zechariah couldn't speak, her friends didn't understand and there wasn't a birthing class for pregnant old ladies she could join. There are times when you may feel alone, but God's timing is perfect and if we prioritise him, he will prioritise us. He will always connect you with the right help at just the right time.

Mary's Response

Have you ever watched those old cowboy films where the bad guys are gaining ground and the good guys are tired, under pressure and losing the strength to fight? Then you hear a sound in the distance, it is the cavalry and they are on their way to help with the final push to secure the victory. There is a heavenly cavalry that God will send to our lives at pivotal moments when we are feeling a little overwhelmed at what we face, and for Elizabeth this was where Mary came in.

Gabriel came to tell Mary that God wanted to use her life to carry Jesus. Just put yourself in her shoes for a moment. She had to face the shame of a teenage pregnancy. She had to explain that this was going to be a virgin birth and that her child was actually the son of God. It was a lot to take in but Mary's capacity and faith were amazing.

I find it so beautiful that along with the news of her pregnancy, Gabriel also told Mary about her cousin Elizabeth, who had entered her sixth month of pregnancy. Why did he give her that information? Surely Mary already had enough to cope with without having to think about Elizabeth as well. But Mary responded immediately. She said to God, 'Let it be! I will carry this child, I am up for this challenge.' In the very next moment she stepped into Elizabeth's shoes. Luke says, *'Mary didn't wait a minute. She got up and travelled to a town in Judah in the hill country, straight to Zechariah's house, and greeted Elizabeth'* (Luke 1:39, The Message).

In Her Shoes

This young, pregnant teenager took a risky and difficult journey to be with Elizabeth after receiving her own life changing news. She went to stand alongside her cousin and support her in her pregnancy. If I was Mary, I think the last thing on my mind would be going to support Elizabeth. I would be consumed with thinking about the challenges my own pregnancy was going to create, but Mary put her own needs aside and reached out.

This is what the life of someone who is committed to walking the shoes of others looks like. They don't just respond to fulfil their personal call, they are also willing to help others reach for theirs. Mary stayed with Elizabeth for three months and I am sure she played a crucial role in helping bring John into the world. What an incredible picture that is, Jesus was in Mary's womb as she helped to prepare the way for the preparer of his way!

The Leap

It says, *'When Elizabeth heard Mary's greeting, the baby leaped in her womb, and Elizabeth was filled with the Holy Spirit. In a loud voice she exclaimed: "Blessed are you among women and blessed is the child you will bear! But why am I so favoured, that the mother of my Lord should come to me? As soon as the sound of your greeting reached my ears, the baby in my womb leaped for joy." '*

(Luke 1:41 - 44)

God wants you to know that there is a Mary for every Elizabeth. There are people he will send to walk alongside you when you commit to step out for the benefit of others. I have had the absolute joy of bumping into some Marys on my journey. They are precious friends who have joined my life at just the right time. They have come alongside me as I have been making a stretch and committed to step out by launching a new project. They have encouraged me and spoken up when Zechariah has been silent. When you meet a Mary your heart will leap as your worlds connect, just like Jesus and John leaped in their mothers' wombs. I have committed to be a Mary to those God puts on my heart. I don't want to be so consumed with what I am doing that I miss the opportunity to help others. Every time I have taken my eyes off my own needs and been there for others something very special has happened. I have many friendships with people who live oceans apart, and yet whenever we are together our hearts leap. But these kinds of relationships only happen once you say 'yes'. Mary and Elizabeth both had to have a 'yes' moment before their lives were brought together. If you're praying for help and it's not coming, maybe your 'yes' is the trigger that will make it happen.

So if you feel God stretching you, but like Zechariah you are unsure and a little fearful, then don't worry. Let your questions be silenced and trust God because your journey is just beginning. God let Zechariah name John, it took a while but he reached a place of faith and stepped out. Don't fear the unknown or worry about the inconvenience. If God is speaking to you it's because he knows you are more than capable.

Maybe you are like Elizabeth. You are up for the challenge and you are incubating some ideas that will end up helping many others. Stay strong, focus on the joy of what this expansion will do for you and others, and look out for Mary. Or maybe you are like Mary and are making the journey to give your life away to those around you. Whichever person you most relate to, remember that God's main concern is the arrival of that baby. He cares about all the people your 'yes' response is going to help.

In Her Shoes

So dear friend, I am praying that as you have read this book you have been strengthened and inspired. I pray that it has been a source of encouragement and confirmation for you to keep stretching and growing. I close by simply asking whose world can you enter? Which priorities do you need to change and how far can you stretch? You are God's answer for your neighbourhood, community and beyond, so I suggest that you put this book down, go out, and try on some more shoes.

THERE WERE NO SHOES
JESUS WOULDN'T STEP INTO

NO WORLD HIS LOVE
COULDN'T REACH

CHAPTER 9

IN THEIR SHOES

Over the next few pages there are incredible stories from some amazing, beautiful women. These women are opening the pages of their life to share their story with you and are inviting you to step into their shoes. The shoes of the lonely, abused and broken. Shoes similar to the ones so many women in our world are wearing today.

Their stories show that no-one has gone too far to be rescued, there is no wound that God can't heal, and there is no life that he can't use. I thank every one of these women for writing their story so that others can also find their freedom.

I pray that as you read about their journeys your compassion will grow, your heart will be encouraged and your commitment to reach out will be strengthened.

In Her Shoes

These women's stories would not have had a happy ending if someone hadn't stepped out and made room for them in their world. I hope that as you read, it will encourage you to see what you can do for someone else.

We all have a story. What is yours and how can you use it to reach out to others?

Be inspired as you walk for a while in their shoes!

In Her Shoes

In The Shoes... Of The Abused

As a child I always wanted to be involved in the performing arts. I knew from being young that it was what I wanted to do with my life. But my dreams and confidence were snatched from me by sexual abuse. I desperately tried to cover up what had happened and erase the painful memories which haunted me. No matter how hard I tried I couldn't get over it and the only escape I could find was in alcohol so I started to get drunk on wine and spirits every weekend.

I left home and went to university but my problems continued to deepen and my lifestyle became more destructive. Before long I moved on from alcohol to drugs. It was my way of blotting out the pain but it soon started to control my life. I developed a cocaine habit and dropped out of university to start working full-time as a prostitute in an attempt to satisfy my drug addiction. By the age of nineteen I found myself far away from my dreams, trapped in a world of sin, lies and abuse.

During this time I had a baby, a beautiful little boy who was, and still is the most precious thing in my life. I moved in with his Dad in an attempt to create the perfect family that I had always longed for. Our relationship didn't work out and I quickly turned back to prostitution to make ends meet. I got used to being abused for money and started taking even more drugs to cover up the hurt I felt inside.

My friends were all caught up in the same lifestyle so we understood each other. But those on the outside had no idea what it was like to be me, I felt so isolated and alone.

A few months later I hit rock bottom and it could have been the end of my story if it hadn't been for my Aunt who reached out to me. She has always had a positive influence on my life and I could remember going to her house as a child and feeling so loved and secure. My Aunt invited me to go to church with her, but that was the last place on earth I thought a girl like me would be welcome. I thought Christians would judge me for my lifestyle and try to force the Bible on me. In the end I agreed because she was the only person who had ever shown such genuine concern for me, and I trusted her.

In Her Shoes

The first time I went to church God took hold of my hand and my life has never been the same since. He saved me and I have never taken cocaine or sold my body since that day. I got another chance at life, and my decision also meant that my son now has a brighter future. Just a few months after I was saved, I was accepted onto the Abundant Life Leadership Academy in Bradford and I have never looked back.

I am now part of the 'red light ministry' at the church. We go out a few times a week to reach out to the prostitutes on the streets of our city. That used to be me, but now I can step into their shoes, love them and help them walk into the same freedom I have found. I know that their lives can change, just like mine!

I'm determined to keep on living my 'once upon a time' the way God has planned it for me. I can dream again and aspire to great things in life, and I just can't wait to see what will come next!

Simone

In Her Shoes

In The Shoes... Of The Includer

'People are precious!' An old lady who stayed with our family for a few years used to walk around saying it all the time, and she was right. People are precious, they are the most treasured and valuable part of God's creation, and I guess that is why my life has unfolded in the way it has.

Our story started around twenty three years ago, when my husband and I bought a massive twelve bedroom house. As a family of five we certainly didn't need that much space, but we didn't buy it for us. We felt that God had told us to expand our lives for the sake of others.

For quite some time before then we had started to noticed the overwhelming needs of those around us and we felt challenged to be part of the answer. We saw young people who had left home and needed a safe place to stay, we saw vulnerable old people who desperately wanted someone to value them, overseas students who were thrown into a foreign culture and needed help settling in and the parents of disabled youngsters who needed a break from looking after their children. We saw people from all walks of life who were in need of someone to step into their shoes and care enough about them to reach out. We took the decision to open up the door of our home, to include and love people, and we have never looked back. Our house was always full. We usually had between twelve and twenty people for lunch every Sunday and many people stayed with us for extended periods of time. Some were students, others were elderly people who needed a loving home where they were cherished.

I have to say that enlarging our hearts and opening our home in this way has not been without its challenges. Financially it was costly, and to be honest we really couldn't afford it, but what we had always seemed to stretch. We always had enough and I guess that is what happens when you put God first, he takes care of you.

Over the years my husband and I started to reach further afield after we caught a real heart for Africa. We have developed a great relationship with a church out in Kenya and visit every year to encourage them.

On our last visit we set up a People Empowering People (PEP) group which helps support small businesses. We have also had the privilege of working with disadvantaged people and were able to meet some of their practical needs by giving them food parcels. It might not sound like much, but to some it's a real lifeline. One woman who attended this meeting had planned to commit suicide by swallowing poison because she didn't feel her life was worth living anymore. She ended up going to church the next Sunday and got saved. Sometimes we can think that we can't do much, but I have seen that when we just do something, God uses it in a way we couldn't have imagined.

Another of our passions is to empower others and help them take that same step to enlarge their lives and reach out. On each visit to Africa we take volunteers with us who want to use their skills and abilities to help the local community. It's such a joy for us to watch as they start to connect with people from a totally different culture to their own and learn to walk in other people's shoes.

In Her Shoes

I have definitely discovered that whenever you do things for others, you get a far greater sense of satisfaction than when you just look out for yourself. Sometimes it can mean you have to go even further than the extra mile, you have to go the fourth, fifth and even the tenth mile at times. It is inconvenient and it isn't always easy, but I can promise you that it will enrich your life immeasurably. It's true that you can't help everyone, but you can always help someone. So I want to encourage you to look around you and start to make a difference. Who can you reach out to today?

Sharon

In Her Shoes

In The Shoes... Of The Stranger

I was born in the Congo, a country torn apart by war. It was often a dangerous place to be and I can remember once having to hide under a table with my Mum, who was heavily pregnant at the time, because we could hear gunfire outside. The situation was so bad that my Mum needed bodyguards to protect her on the way to the hospital when she gave birth to my brother.

We moved from the Congo to South Africa when I was six years old because my Dad wanted us to have a decent education. We had no idea at the time about the terrible atrocities being committed in the neighbouring country of Rwanda as the genocide unfolded there. We left just before the trouble spilled over into the Congo and this was the timing of God for our family. My mum is from the Tutsi tribe and it was her people who were being slaughtered. My father is Congolese and from a different tribe so their marriage would have been seen as treason and all our lives could have been lost in the violence.

In Her Shoes

About seven years later we moved once more, this time to England, but my father stayed behind in Africa for a year to work. Arriving in England was a total shock for me and it was a very difficult experience. My first few months were traumatic as I tried to adapt to a brand new culture and way of life. It was so different to Africa and I am sad to say that I found the climate cold, and the welcome we received from people even colder. I felt lonely and isolated as I tried desperately to fit into my new surroundings.

A few months later we started to attend a local church and this was when our lives began to improve. The Pastor and his family could see we were struggling and they stepped into our shoes and started to support us in very practical ways. They found us somewhere to live and helped us through the difficult process of adapting to life in a new country. They got alongside us, loved us and accepted us. This meant more than they will ever know. Other people at the church also helped us to settle in and finally feel at home. It was a precious gift to us.

In Her Shoes

This was many years ago, but my experiences have made me very aware of other people who might feel lonely and isolated like I did back then. It has made me look out for the stranger and has inspired me to reach out to others, especially those who are trying to find their feet in a new country or city. I have learned that when someone chooses to step into your shoes it can make a massive difference to your life, and now I want to do the same for others.

Anaïs

In Her Shoes

In The Shoes… Of The Poor

I've had a great, stable upbringing in a loving, Christian home. It's all I have ever known and I'm so grateful for that. But sometimes if you have a background like mine you can end up thinking that you have less of a story to tell. It makes it difficult to see how you can relate to people who have experienced a totally different side of life. I mean how can a good Christian girl like me relate to the broken, the abused or the drug addict when I have no idea what it is to be in their situation?

Over the past few years I have discovered that you can relate to all kinds of people, it's not about your background, it's about your heart to reach out and do whatever you can. It started when I got a job as a graphic designer with Christians Against Poverty (CAP). They are an awesome charity who help people facing financial difficulties get out of debt. Working at CAP has connected my life to people who have been totally desperate, ready to take their own life and unable to face another day. As I have heard their heartbreaking stories God has stretched my heart and given me greater compassion for others. Through my job I get to produce brochures and magazines that help them tell their story and encourage others to get involved in reaching out. I find it such a privilege because Jesus loved the poor and made them a priority, and that is what I get to do every day. I also see people saved regularly through the work we do around the world which is amazing!

If you think that you can't relate to someone then I want to encourage you to try stepping into their shoes. I have found that you don't need to have been through the same experiences, you just need to care enough to reach out and make a difference.

Claire

In The Shoes... Of A Survivor

I married Geoff when I was twenty two, and from the start I had a strong sense that we should foster and adopt children before we had our own. I started to look into it, but people around us strongly advised us not to. They just didn't think it was a good idea. A few months later after trying for a family, we were told we could never have children. The news was devastating because I had always wanted to have a family. I felt such a deep sense of grief for the children that would never be mine.

Not long after we received the news, I was sat in church when I felt God speaking into my heart. At first I thought it was just my imagination, but then the preacher got up and spoke exactly the same words that had just come into my head. He gave me a picture of a house with big windows and lots of children in it. Funnily enough that is the house I live in now!

A few years later our desire for a family was as strong as ever so we started looking into adoption. The door to our dream opened and we became the proud parents of three gorgeous children who were from the same family. It has been one of the best, but also one of the hardest things we have ever done. Without going into detail our children weren't the average package and they had a difficult history. Those first few months were such a challenge as we learned to adapt, and to love unconditionally. Nine months after adopting our first three we got a call from Social Services saying that their birth mum was pregnant again. We took on the baby when he was just six weeks old so that he could be raised with his siblings. Around the same time we moved to Bradford and after a search we settled at an amazing church. Finally I was in a place where I could flourish and grow. We had a great life, a beautiful family and were looking forward to the future.

Life does not always go as you have planned and in June 2007 my life changed forever. One day I went to my Grandfather's funeral, on the next day my husband was given his redundancy notice, and the day after that I was told the devastating news that I had cancer. The doctors had found a 'scattering' of fast growing tumours around my heart. Without treatment I had only a few months left to live. As the gravity of my situation began to sink in I knew I had to go straight to God and start to focus on his truth. I read the verse in Mark 11 which says, 'I tell you the truth, if anyone says to this mountain, 'Go, throw yourself into the sea,' and does not doubt in his heart but believes that what he says will happen, it will be done for him' (Mark 11:23). God reassured me that he was there and that I just needed to go through the treatment.

One week later I started a course of chemotherapy and nothing could have prepared me for the terrible effects it would have on me. I felt so unwell that often I could barely string four words together. I just couldn't believe this was happening to me. But one day I was sitting in God's presence and I felt him say that this could be the best day of my life if I lived it with him. From that moment on I decided to make the most of every moment and use my illness as an opportunity to reach others.

I was a regular outpatient on the cancer treatment ward and this placed me in the world of many other people who were seriously ill. I am still amazed at how God has used me to help others during the very lowest and hardest points of my life. I prayed with many people who were seriously ill and believed with them for a miracle. I just wanted to bring a ray of hope into the desperation I knew they felt.

While I was in hospital I met a Muslim lady who was being given very high doses of chemotherapy. One day she broke down and said she couldn't take it anymore. Her distraught family knew that without it she would die, and it was heartbreaking to watch them plead with her to change her mind. Eventually her husband told the nurse that his wife had said she was willing to continue with her treatment if she could have it with, 'that lady', and he pointed in my direction. They didn't even know my name, but he explained that he knew I was different to everyone else because he could see God in me.

We had our next two treatments together. To be honest, it was hard for me because she was so negative about her chances of surviving. When the time came for our next appointment she was too ill to be there. Once she was well enough for another dose of chemo I visited her in hospital and sat with her through it to support her. We are still in touch today as she continues her fight against the disease.

In Her Shoes

I also made friends with a single mum who had a daughter the same age as mine. My husband and I wanted to help her out because we knew that facing cancer together was hard and couldn't imagine how difficult it must have been facing it alone. We got alongside her and offered to help by looking after her daughter one day and night a week to give her a break. Sadly, she didn't make it but we have stayed in contact with her little girl who is now living with her extended family.

My illness helped me step into the shoes of others who faced the same circumstances and I realised that for many women one of the most distressing side-effects of chemotherapy was losing their hair. It shattered their self-confidence and I hated to see what it did to them. I wanted them to know they were still attractive and cherished so I used to spend hours telling them how beautiful they were.

During this awful time, something else that helped keep me going was the support of our amazing friends. They came alongside us, prayed for me and cared for my family.

In Her Shoes

They brought us meals, helped to look after our children and encouraged us if we felt like giving up. Their love and concern helped us so much as we walked through this difficult time together. I am so grateful to have such beautiful friends in my world.

I am now free from cancer, but I have been left with a few after effects from my treatment. Despite this I am confident about the future and am determined to fulfill my destiny. It sounds a bit surreal to say this but I know that through this trial I have been so blessed. I have seen God at work in my life and in the lives of those around me. If you are facing an illness or a difficult situation in your life right now, then I want you to know that you can trust God. No matter how bad it gets and even on your darkest days he is faithful and he can still use what you are going through to reach others.

Cathy

In Her Shoes

In The Shoes… Of The Self-Harmer

Growing up I never felt that I was good enough. I hated myself and I hated my life. By the age of twelve I had started on a downward spiral of bulimia and self-harm, and before long it completely controlled my life. As a teenager I did my best to hide my shameful secret and I soon became an expert at wearing a mask and pretending my life was fine. In reality I felt so torn inside, it was like being two totally different people. I had my public face which tried to show that everything was alright, and then there was the real me which was falling apart. I would gorge myself on food, vomit it back up and then this destructive cycle would start all over again. I felt completely repulsed by my behaviour but I didn't know how to stop and this just added to my sense of self-loathing.

When I was fifteen something happened to me that sent me even further over the edge. I was on holiday and sneaked out late at night to meet some friends at a bar. As I left to go home, two men followed me down the street. They dragged me into a dark alleyway and raped me. I couldn't cope with what had happened and I tried to block it out. Fear, shame and feelings of complete worthlessness started to overwhelm my life and I dealt with it the only way I knew how. By eating everything I could, making myself vomit and by slicing at my skin with a razor blade.

When I was eighteen I moved away to university and hoped that I would be able to escape my past. But it followed me and the bulimia and self-harm tightened its grip. Despite having many friends I felt so alone, because no-one knew what was going on and I didn't think that anyone would understand. It got so bad that I became suicidal and started to plan how I could kill myself. Each night I prayed that I would die in an accident because I was so desperate to escape the pain, and every morning when I woke up my heart was filled with dread at the thought of having to face another day.

I tried to get medical help, but not even doctors could help me. They prescribed various anti-depressants but none of them worked. I was referred to many 'specialists', and was even told by one counsellor that if I didn't pull myself together I would end up being 'put away' in a psychiatric unit for my own protection. This scared me so much that I never went back to see them again after that.

In Her Shoes

A new chapter of my life began when I started attending a church near to where I live. I met some women there who befriended me. They loved me consistently whether I was up or down and this helped me to dismantle some of the barriers I had built up around my life. When I needed encouragement they were there, sending me text messages at just the right moment and inviting me to their homes.

Something that really helped me was that my new friends were willing to tell me their own stories. They had also walked through some difficult situations but they were very open about it and didn't try to hide it like me. I began to realise that I needed to be real about my own life, and felt that I could trust these people enough to be honest with them.

They arranged for me to see a Christian counsellor who was fantastic. The pain inside me was so strong at times that I couldn't even speak and I spent many hours with her just sobbing uncontrollably. I didn't change overnight, but my friends kept on loving me, praying for me and teaching me the truth. They were so patient and refused to give up and helped me to believe that my life could change.

One night I finally reached my lowest point. I was alone in my house and had been bingeing, vomiting and cutting myself for many hours. I sat on my bedroom floor covered in food, blood and vomit, totally disgusted at myself for the state I was in. I felt God whisper to my heart, he just said, 'Enough.' Something broke inside me at that moment. It was as if God's arm reached down and lifted me out of the terrible darkness and desperation that had consumed me for so many years.

That night I listened to a teaching CD by a lady called Nancy Alcorn who runs an organisation called Mercy Ministries. As I heard her talk it was like light bulbs going on in my head and I realised that I had to choose to walk through my prison door to freedom. I have never self-harmed or made myself sick again from that day. It hasn't been easy and there have been many times when I felt as if a huge battle was going on inside of me. These wrong thoughts and behaviours had been part of my life for so long that I didn't know how to exist without them. During this process I learnt to depend on God like never before, and I started to replace all the lies I believed about myself with his truth. I learnt to accept God's love and came to

In Her Shoes

understand that the price of my freedom had already been paid by Jesus when he died on the cross.

Today I am completely free from depression, bulimia and self-harm and I have been released from the shame and despair which dominated my life for so long. I am living proof that God is in the business of transforming lives. But I don't know how my story would have ended if someone hadn't taken the time to walk in my shoes. During my journey the encouragement and concern of those around me kept me going in my darkest moments. Thanks to those who were willing to love and reach out to me, God has healed me and made my life beautiful again. I used to wish my life was over, but now I am a forgiven and cherished daughter of the king!

Amy

In Her Shoes

In The Shoes... Of The Elderly

The word 'dignity' means to be held in high esteem or respect. When you dignify someone you make them feel valued, and I have given my life to restoring the dignity of the elderly. I have a heart for older people, it's something that has burned within me for many years. I am committed to help them see the treasure within their own lives, to place worth on those who feel they are worthless, to love the unloved and embrace the lonely. As I have stepped out and dared to believe God I have seen him do incredible things in the lives of some of the most vulnerable people in our society.

I got my first taste of care for the elderly at the age of seventeen when I was sent on a college placement to a large residential home and was shocked at what I saw. It was so difficult to watch old people suffering, scared, alone and often mistreated. Afterwards I wrote an essay condemning what I had experienced. I vowed that if I was ever in a position to change how they were cared for I would do it!

In Her Shoes

I think it's probably unusual for a teenager to have such a passion for elderly people, but it is the way God has wired me. It is one of my first things and I have dedicated most of my life to looking after the elderly and fighting their cause for them. Injustice makes me so angry and when I see these precious people being mistreated or abused I just can't stand by and watch.

I became a Christian a few years ago in my mid-forties, and not long after this God clearly spoke to me about raising the profile of the elderly in our church. Before long a new ministry called 'Splendour' was born which exists to reach out to older people. Through the work of Splendour we have helped many find God in their final years and even weeks of their lives. None of us know how long we have got, but the window of opportunity to reach someone who is in later life can be narrow, so we have no time to lose. I know that as I reach out, I'm not just changing their life on earth, I'm helping to change their eternal destiny and that is such an incredible privilege.

In Her Shoes

You may find it difficult to step into the shoes of an elderly person and understand what their life is like, so let me share with you some stories about those I have come to love so dearly.

One day I went to pick up some older people to bring them to church. A gentleman stood in front of me proudly wearing his blazer and shirt saying, 'How do I look?' He had made such an effort, but his trousers were stained in urine and his blazer marked with food. He wasn't able to look after himself and wasn't getting the care he needed. It is things like this that break my heart, they keep me awake at night and spur me on to keep reaching out.

The incredible thing I have discovered about God is that when you step into the shoes of others he is there with you. On one occasion I remember our team visiting a home that was dark and stank of stale urine and chip fat. Vulnerable elderly people were living alongside recovering alcoholics and drug users, and some of the older people had mental health problems. Seven old people got saved through us reaching out to them that day. Sometimes all you can do is share God's message of hope and it breaks your heart that you can't do much more to improve their situations. What keeps me going is knowing that although some of them may have lived in difficult circumstances here on earth, God has a beautiful mansion waiting for them in heaven.

Old people are just like you and I. They have a history, they have a story to tell and sometimes hearing it can shock you. Suddenly you don't just see an old person sat in front of you, you see someone who was once a scared child, you see someone who has faced a terrible loss or the intense pain caused by bereavement. One day I was completely broken as one gentleman started to open up and share his story with me. Fifteen years earlier he had been in a house fire and been through the horror of watching his wife burn to death. He had been unable to save her and blamed himself for it. He couldn't face life anymore and had locked himself away from society ever since, until the day we entered his world. As we reached out to him with love and compassion we brought hope into his hopelessness. Now he prays every day and asks God to protect us because his life has changed for the better since we stepped into his shoes. These are just a few of so many stories I could tell you about the old people we have reached out to who are desperately lonely and longing for someone to care enough about them to enter their world.

So often people can see an elderly person and write them off as being 'past it' without stopping to find out anything about them. Old people are just the same as you except they have a few more miles on the clock. Many of them have been through so much in life and yet keep walking. They are a joy to know and connecting your life to theirs is such an enriching experience.

It doesn't take much to enter the world of the elderly. Just being willing to pop in and see them, or taking time out of your busy schedule to share a cup of tea can make their day.

Elderly people are precious and valuable, they deserve to be loved and cherished in their final years on earth. The fact is that one day you will be old, one day you will live in

In Her Shoes

their shoes. Why not value them how you yourself hope to be valued? Instead of walking by, stop for a moment and think about what you can do to reach out to the elderly people in your world.

Christine

In Her Shoes

In The Shoes... Of The Fatherless

My story starts when I was seventeen. Like many teenagers I was starting to discover boys and after making a few bad choices I fell pregnant. It wasn't what I had expected for my life but I soon found myself as a young single mum facing all the challenges that brings. I got married a few years later but it didn't last and I found myself alone once more, bringing up my two beautiful girls. My life changed when I struck up a friendship with a great guy who was also a single parent. I supported him as he battled cancer and miraculously survived. Our friendship deepened and we fell in love and got married a few years later. We were told it wasn't possible for us to have our own children because of my husband's illness, but at the time it didn't matter because we had our own ready made family. Despite this I still had a deep desire to have another baby, but I thought it was just a dream.

Our lives changed in the year 2000 when we joined a great church. Our attitudes and our thinking were challenged and we grew in our faith. It was at this time that my dream of having a baby started to stir in my heart once again. I knew that God was a miracle worker, and although the doctors said it couldn't happen, it was still possible. We started to believe for our child. Years went by and there was no sign of our baby, but I kept believing because I knew that this was a 'God dream' in my heart. I remember reading the scripture in Isaiah 54 that says, 'Sing, O barren woman, you who never bore a child: burst into song, shout for joy' (Isaiah 54:1). So I did what it said and continued to trust God.

At the time I was working in a pre-school nursery. My heart was drawn to one particular little girl who attended the sessions. She was looked after by the social care system and had a very sad story and difficult background. Being around her moved my heart, there just was something about her that got to me. It didn't take much to step into her shoes and see how alone she was in life and that what she needed most was a family to belong to. One day I was chatting to a colleague about this little girl and they suggested the possibility of me adopting her. I just laughed it off at the time because I wanted to get pregnant myself and have my own baby, not take on someone else's. Despite this, a seed had been planted in my heart and I started to think about adopting a child and asked God if this was the right way forward. We felt totally at peace about it as a couple so we started to look into the adoption process and believed that if it was right for us then the door would open.

During this time we went through many personal challenges and our patience was sorely tested as the months dragged on. In June 2006 we were accepted to adopt a child. As a family we were very excited, but it was another six months until we got the phone call that we had been hoping for. There was a little girl aged three who desperately needed a family. We read the background information about her and fell in love with her without even seeing a photo.

The day we finally met our daughter was amazing. Our beautiful little girl ran to meet us calling us Mummy and Daddy. The baby God promised us had arrived after all our years of waiting, praying and dreaming. I am so grateful to God because his plans are always better than our own and he always keeps his promises. Adopting our daughter has been an amazing experience for us and I want to encourage other people to consider it. There are so

In Her Shoes

many beautiful children out there that are totally alone, they just need someone to care, they are waiting for someone to reach out to them and step into their shoes. Maybe you could be the one to make a difference to their life.

Helen

In Her Shoes

In The Shoes... Of The Addict

I grew up a 'good' kid with parents who loved me and wanted me to be all that I could possibly be, but I didn't know Jesus. When I was a teenager I started to experiment with life and was into boys, drinking and parties. I went to university I started dating a guy there who was a heroin addict. I thought I could help him and change him but I was wrong. I fell pregnant and chose to have an abortion. This was the beginning of a very difficult time for me that saw me go from taking 'party' drugs on weekends to being a hard-core heroin addict. I became filled with so much shame, guilt and anger that I dropped out of university. The addiction was stronger than I was and I couldn't escape it. The drugs stopped the pain momentarily and then the struggle was on again to do whatever was necessary to get more heroin. At the age of twenty one I got fired from my regular job after stealing large amounts of money from them. I was told that I had to go to rehab or jail. I fooled them into thinking rehab was the best option for me, but that same night I started selling my body (and soul) on the streets to strangers to get my drug money. I can tell you that prostitution is not like the film 'Pretty Woman.' It was the darkest, most soul destroying time of my life.

In Her Shoes

Then one night as I was getting ready for 'work' my Mum showed up. She came back into my life at the moment that I needed someone the most. She cried a lot and told me that I was not the girl that she had raised me to be. My Mum challenged me look in the mirror and ask myself who I was. The thought of doing this scared me because at that point I was a prostitute with a drug addiction. I only weighed 40kg, had brown skin hanging off my bones and I looked like death warmed up. As I looked at my reflection, it was a sobering moment. I didn't know who I was. I didn't know how I had ended up in such a mess and I had no idea how to get out of it. I decided that I had to do something to try and change my life so one day I simply ran away from the underworld of drugs and prostitution. I attempted to get off the drugs in my own strength. It never worked and I lasted a week before deciding that I deserved a treat and took some more heroin.

My life changed when I met a man who wanted to help me, not just use me like all the others. He was a doctor who treated drug addicts and I went to see him, not knowing he was a Christian. He told me I had a hole in my soul that only Jesus could fill, not drugs, or sex. To be honest I thought he was crazy! But he encouraged me to go back into rehab – but this time to a Christian rehab.

I agreed and I managed to stay off the drugs during my time there, but I was rude, nasty, and rebellious towards those trying to help me. These kind Christian people would offer to pray for me, and I would colourfully tell them 'No!' Six weeks into the program I was still clean from drugs but very lost, sad and lonely.

The people running the course wanted me to go to church but I refused. One Sunday it was pouring with rain and I had nowhere to smoke my cigarettes so I went into a service. The congregation sang their 'Jesus music' and then the Pastor preached a message about the burden removing, yoke destroying power of God. I don't remember making a decision to go to the front but before I knew it I was there with my hands raised, tears falling and crying out to God for help. He wrapped his loving arms of grace, mercy and forgiveness around me and I knew this was a new start. That was 1999 and I have had an amazing roller coaster ride with Jesus ever since!

In Her Shoes

My life today couldn't be more different. I am married to a loving, supportive husband called Jason, and we have three of the world's most gorgeous little girls called Grace, Rebekah and Lauryn.

I wanted to take my story and make it count by using it to reach others, so I started a charity here in Australia called the 'Hope Foundation.' It exists to bring hope, help and healing to other hurting young women from a similar background to me. I want them to know that they are loved, valued and created for a purpose. It has been such a joy to see many lives turned around by God's great love and forgiveness. My life story has been published in a book called 'Trophy of Grace', and I preach about God's unending love all over the place. I used to be a drug addicted prostitute who had no hope and no future, but now I am a hope bearer, a grace sharer and living a life that has been radically transformed.

Bronwen

www.hopefoundation.org.au
www.trophyofgrace.com

IN HER SHOES

In Their Shoes... For A Lifetime

I once asked my mother Elsie, why she had such a concern for other people even though she had been through a difficult childhood herself. She used to say, 'That was my life, but now I can make life better for other people!' This is a motto that has lasted her entire lifetime, and at the grand age of ninety four she is still reaching out to others.

She didn't have the easiest of starts in life and lost her own mother at the age of ten when she died following a long illness. This was the end of her carefree childhood because as the eldest girl she ended up looking after her father and older brother. Elsie was expected to do all the household chores and spent hours cooking, cleaning and doing the laundry. It was such a lot for a child to cope with, but she did not let it affect her. She sees her experiences as a reason to try and help others, so they don't have to go through what she did.

She has consistently put others first and used to work as a nurse orderly on a ward for patients who were terminally ill or suffered from chronic illnesses. It was so much more than a job to her, and she always went the extra mile by

In Her Shoes

being extra gentle when changing their dressings. Elsie even went to visit patients after they had left hospital, to see how they were getting on. It wasn't part of her job it was just something she chose to do. I know that she brightened up the world of so many lonely people. She was constantly stepping into their shoes and making others the main priority for her life.

In the 1950's Elsie and my dad, William, moved to Morecambe. It was here that she spent several years working for a Bradford based charity called Cinderella Homes. The organization reached out to the poorest and neediest children in the city, giving them food, clothing and even organizing for them to go on holiday. Elsie was part of a team that ran a Cinderella Home in Morecambe, and later helped to look after more than fifty children at a time as the matron of a holiday camp. She was always willing to expand her heart to make room for more people, her love could always stretch that bit further and the children loved her for it.

Even today Elsie continues to give to others. She always has a smile and a kind word for those that cross her path. She is still reaching out and gracing the world of others with her kindness. She loves people and embraces them all, the young and the old, the rich and the poor. It is her natural reaction to reach out and I think she has walked in the shoes of others for so long that she doesn't even have to think about it anymore It is just who she is and what she does.

I hope that Elsie's story inspires you to see that reaching others is a lifestyle that we can all choose. If you have had a difficult background then don't let it hold you back, let it motivate you to help others just like Elsie did. Perhaps no-one stepped into your world when you needed them, but now you can be the answer for someone else. You can reach out your hand and breathe hope into their world, you can be the encouragement they long for and make a difference to their lives.

In Her Shoes

Elsie is such a beautiful lady and she continues to light up the lives of those she touches every day. She has left a legacy of kindness behind her as she has walked through life and we can do the same. But to follow in her footsteps, you will need to start stepping into someone else's shoes.

Barbara

**STEPPING INTO THE
SHOES OF OTHERS**

**WILL CHANGE
YOUR LIFE
FOREVER**

Get Involved

Maybe after reading this book your heart is stirred to do more to reach outside of your world and walk in the shoes of others. There are many ways you can do this, just start where you live with the people around you.

I want to share some of the practical ways I have found to make a real difference. The next few pages tell you about some amazing opportunities which are close to my heart, and can help you walk in other people's shoes.

In Her Shoes

In Their Shoes With

Compassion
Releasing children from poverty in Jesus' name

Compassion is an amazing charity that goes to parts of the world where you and I may never go, to developing nations, where they find the broken, the lost and the orphan. They feel their hurt and experience first hand their lack and from that place of love and understanding, they extend an invitation to you and I to practically walk in the shoes of some incredible children.

We sponsor several children as a family, and thousands as a church. It is a life changing experience, and for just a small contribution each month you can take care of a child's physical and spiritual needs. You can help feed, clothe and teach them. You can write to your child on a regular basis and even arrange to go and meet them.

Please consider walking in the shoes of one of these children by becoming a sponsor. You can make a difference today.

For more information visit: **www.compassion.com**

IN HER SHOES

IN THEIR SHOES WITH

Mercy Ministries
valuing every young woman's future

I met Nancy Alcorn, the founder and president of Mercy Ministries over ten years ago. She is one of my heroes, she has given her life to walking in the shoes of young girls who are broken, hurting and abused.

Nancy loves these girls who the government can't rehabilitate and the world can only medicate. She has given her life to building homes where they can attend a programme free of charge. Homes where they can find real answers and the unconditional love of God. A place where they are not judged, but walk to a place of restoration and freedom. These Mercy homes are now all over the world and you can help a hurting girl by partnering with this amazing ministry.

For more information visit **www.mercyministries.org**

In Her Shoes

In Their Shoes With

CHERISH FOUNDATION

This ministry is very special to me. I started it after hearing God whisper to my heart several years ago and tell me to do something to honour and place value on those who feel they are not valued. To celebrate those who have never felt celebrated and to step into the shoes of the victim, the betrayed, the abused and create a place where they can see just how loved they are. A place where we let them know they are not alone and rally an army of women to cheer them on.

Each year at our Cherish women's conference we devote an evening to do just that. We tell the story of how different ones have walked through trials and survived, and then we present them with amazing gifts to say 'We believe in you.' From cars to once in a life time holidays we give something that will bless their world. For many it's the first time they have experienced that kind of generosity and sense of value. The Foundation is made possible by the generosity of women who give each year to this great cause.

For more information and to find out how you can attend one of these evenings visit: **www.alm.org.uk/cherish**

By the same Author:

identity

This book is about a journey, one that I believe we must all embark upon, and one that confronts you with the question, 'Who Am I?'

If you would answer this question with a title, label or role that you currently fulfil in life, then think again. This journey requires you to dig much deeper than that and find out what makes you unique; it is all about discovering the real you.

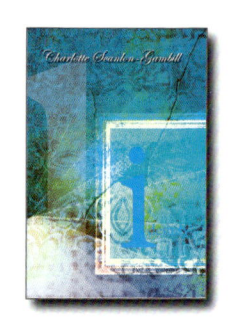

We only have one life, so we need to make sure that our journey gets everything out of us that God intended. Your journey of identity is not always an easy one to take because it demands that you separate from things that send you on a detour relationally, emotionally, mentally and spiritually. But it will connect your life to new opportunities and relationships that are more in keeping with who you really are.

So, wherever you are at on your journey, this book will challenge you to look intently at your life. It will be an indispensable travel guide to help you find your way to the 'real you'.

In Her Shoes

By the same Author:

believe?

So you are saved, you are part of God's family and a child of the King. That might be what you 'say' but how much of it do you actually believe?

I have come to realise that there is an epidemic of 'unbelieving Believers' across the church today. People who love God and believe 'in God' but don't really 'believe God'. Belief is always expressed through doing and there is so much they need to get on and 'do'. For them doubt and unbelief has become a handbrake on their lives, locking up their potential and limiting their usefulness.

This book will challenge every Believer to eradicate unbelief and ask, 'am I using everything God untrusted to my world? Do I believe his Word over my life?'

The truth is, God believes in you and all of heaven is behind you. the question is, do you believe?

IN HER SHOES

By the same Author:

Consumer or Consumed?

David wrote, 'Zeal for your House consumes me.' So what about you?

In every House there are two types of people, consumers and the consumed. Over the years, God's House has been given a bad reputation because it has served the consumers of church life and marginalized those with a genuine zeal.

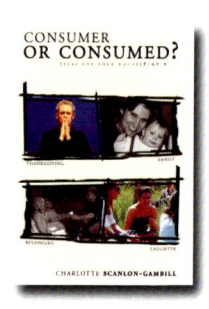

In this challenging and insightful book, Charlotte takes a look 'through the keyhole' to explore just what we should be seeing and hearing in God's House, and shares practical wisdom to equip everyone involved in building the church today.

This book includes a specially created DVD with video tracks demonstrating the consumed heart of the Abundant Life Church.

FURTHER RESOURCES:

For more information about Abundant Life Ministries, conferences and teaching resources by Pastor Charlotte Scanlon-Gambill visit our online store or contact:

Abundant Life Church
Wapping Road, Bradford
West Yorkshire BD3 0EQ

Tel: +44 (0)1274 307233
Fax: +44 (0)1274 740698
Email: admin@alm.org.uk

Visit our online store at **www.alm.org.uk/shop**

Editorial Services from Big Sky Creative

Tel: +44 (0) 1274 724009
info@bigskycreative.co.uk
www.bigskycreative.co.uk